George B Herbert

Anecdotes of the Rebellion

George B Herbert

Anecdotes of the Rebellion

ISBN/EAN: 9783337210687

Printed in Europe, USA, Canada, Australia, Japan

Cover: Foto ©ninafisch / pixelio.de

More available books at **www.hansebooks.com**

ANECDOTES

OF THE

REBELLION.

Compiled and Arranged by

GEORGE B. HERBERT.

Copyrighted, 1894, by
Mast, Crowell & Kirkpatrick.

PUBLISHED BY
MAST, CROWELL & KIRKPATRICK,
SPRINGFIELD, OHIO.

ANECDOTES OF THE REBELLION.

In Southern Prisons.—William H. D. Green, of the 141st Regiment, Pennsylvania Volunteers, was captured September 15, 1863, and remained a prisoner of the rebels until the close of the war. His varied experiences are narrated by himself as follows:

"On the night General Meade broke camp I took the train to Fox's Ford, on the Rappahannock. The next morning Quartermaster Tallman ordered me back to Sulphur Springs to bring on some condemned stock that had been left there the night before. When I got there the picket line had been cut and the stock scattered. I had been busy all day until just at night. Had picked up seventeen, and started to Warrenton Junction to turn them over to the proper authorities. When I got to Fayetteville, about half way between Warrenton and Warrenton Junction, night came on, and as we supposed we were within our own lines we halted, tied our stock in a little piece of woods and encamped for the night; and that night, September 15, 1863, we were captured by a party of Moseby's men, under command of Lieutenant Smith.

"We were immediately marched back through Warrenton, over Flint Hill, and for four days got nothing to eat but a plate of cabbage and a piece of corn bread. September 20, we reached Orange Court House, where we were placed in the common jail for two nights and the intervening day. From there we were sent to Richmond, where we were examined and everything we had taken from us, and then were put into an old tobacco warehouse, known as 'Libby Prison.'

"We staid there about six weeks. A difficulty having arisen between the prisoners, the New York conscripts and the regular soldiers, the latter were sent to Belle Island, where we remained until February, 1864. Here we suffered terribly from the cold. Ice froze twelve inches thick on the James

River. The inhabitants said they had never seen such severe weather there before. Some froze to death, others froze their limbs and died from the effects of amputation.

"It was rumored that there were cases of small-pox in the prison, and the Confederate authorities issued an order that none should have rations except those who would allow themselves to be vaccinated. In a short time hundreds were dying from the effects of sore arms—the disease extending to the entire body and attended with great pain, proved fatal in a majority of cases. Matthew Howe (Company E, captured October, 1863), Elisha W. Parks (corporal in Company D, captured at Gettysburg, July 2, 1863) and myself, as soon as we were vaccinated, stepped out of sight, scratched all the virus off our arms, causing the wound to bleed freely; consequently we suffered but little inconvenience on that account, but did suffer severely from the cold and short rations. Through the Sanitary Commission several bales of clothing and blankets were sent to the prison for the use of prisoners, but the enemy kept the most of them.

"Some of the Confederate officers had dogs which used to come into our camp. At one time when rations were short we killed three of these dogs, buried their heads and skins, and ate the meat with a relish, and looked for more dogs.

"About the 18th or 20th of February we were told we were about to be exchanged, taken out of prison and put in box cars and started, as we supposed, toward the Federal lines; but, alas! instead of that we were taken to Andersonville, where we arrived about the 1st of March, and remained until the 8th of September.

"During our stay here we were literally starved. The only shelters we had were holes dug into the ground and covered with sticks. The camp was very filthy and the prisoners died at the rate of from forty to seventy-five per day. The long-continued confinement and the want of vegetable diet brought on scurvy. In many instances men lost all of their teeth, and gangrene following ate the flesh off their bones. Men were to be seen in whom the entire jawbone back to the ear would thus be exposed before death came to the relief of the sufferer.

"Among the conscripts from New York, drafted at the time of the riots, were a number of desperate characters who allowed themselves to be captured by the enemy at the first opportunity, and some of them were sent to Andersonville. They would steal the rations of their fellow prisoners, and in some cases men were found murdered and stripped of everything they had. Six of these desperadoes were arrested, and tried by a jury of thirty-six men, and formally convicted. The proceedings were sent to the President of the United States, who indorsed the action and approved the verdict of the jury, and the men were hanged the 11th of July, 1864.

"We were kept at Andersonville until the 8th of September, when we were sent to Savannah, where we remained for about a month and then were placed in a stockade about half-way between Savannah and Macon, known as the Millen prison. The inclosure contained about forty acres. About December 1st Sherman drove us out of it, and the same night we were taken out, his men burned the stockade. The next morning we were sent back to Savannah and up the Gulf Railroad, and camped in the woods at various places in Thomas County, but were returned to Andersonville in time to take our Christmas dinner on a very scanty allowance of boiled rice.

"A soldier by the name of Walker had been left sick at Andersonville, got better, and was allowed to go out on his parole not to escape until properly exchanged. He had some little chance to obtain cornmeal, which he used to smuggle into the prison for us, so that we had a little more to eat for the rest of the time we remained there.

"On the 17th of April, 1865, we were taken out for exchange. We were sent by cars to Albany, Georgia, then marched through Thomas County into Florida, turned loose and told to go to Jacksonville, where we arrived April 29, 1865. When about seven miles from Jacksonville, we were met by a squad of our own men with a full supply of bread and coffee, and a reasonable amount of 'commissary.' It is needless to say that we ate with a relish. When we reached camp we had a hard struggle to keep from eating too much. Many of our men were made sick, and some died from over-eating.

"I was almost blind, and went to the surgeon in charge of the Government post there and told him my story. He inquired as to my usual weight; I told him two hundred pounds. He directed me to be weighed and my weight was one hundred and nineteen pounds. He said I was very much reduced in flesh, and the cause of my partial blindness was weakness of the optic nerve produced by poverty of food and ordered me to drink a pint of fresh beef's blood each day. This I did and my sight began to improve.

"We remained at Jacksonville until the 1st of June, when we were put on shipboard for Annapolis, Maryland. After remaining there a few days we were sent to Harrisburg, where we received our discharge, dated June 10, 1865, with three months' extra pay, and were sent home, satisfied that the war was not a failure; that if the Confederacy were not good feeders, nevertheless this was a great and a glorious Union."

The Thrilling Story of a Union Spy.—"Can it be possible that this is Colonel Travers?" exclaimed a middle-aged man to a somewhat older gentleman who was seated before an open fireplace in the office of one of the principal hotels in Portland, Maine. The pensive attitude of the gentleman addressed suddenly gave way to a hearty and enthusiastic welcome, as the younger man made himself known as Captain Blake, formerly of the ——th Regiment, Maine Volunteers.

The writer, seeing the impulsive greeting on the part of each, concluded at once from their military titles that they had been in the service, and at some time in the past had been more than ordinary friends. Hearing Captain Blake express after a few minutes of general conversation great regret at being obliged to leave on account of an engagement and at the same time making an appointment to meet his friend an hour later at the same place to talk over old times, the writer concluded an excellent opportunity was at hand to hear a good story, and, determining not to miss being an auditor if he could help it, took up a paper and waited patiently within a convenient corner, which partially hid him from the colonel's sight, until the captain's return.

Ten minutes after the appointed hour Captain Blake came in, his face aglow with hasty exercise, and, joining his newly-found friend by the fireside, they commenced their conversation. After the captain had told how he passed through the contest without a scratch, and since the war had been successfully farming in the suburbs of Portland, Colonel Travers gave a remarkable history in the following words:

"I have learned since I came North several weeks ago that it has always been the impression among the military circles here that I was hung as a spy or shot dead while trying to run the lines. That report was even made officially, but my presence here ought to be enough to discredit it. But when I look back over the past and think of the months I passed at Castle Thunder, it seems like a horrible dream, to which, for a second experience, death would be vastly preferable. But as you do not know the way I happened to get caught, I will begin my story back when we last met, two weeks before the second 'Bull Run.'

"After that fight had been ended, you will recollect that many new recruits were hurried into the field, especially after it was learned that Lee had crossed into Maryland. The day of the battle of Antietam, fearing the new men might not be relied upon to fill a critical position, my command was posted on the line near the river bank, and I was thus able to get from all sides the best kind of an idea the way the fight was going. At the close of the first day, believing the Confederates to be pretty well broken up, and being strongly impressed with the idea that they would not give another battle in the position they then were, I offered to go across the river and secure, if possible, their future plans, knowing it was vitally important that we should learn something of their movements and exact location, before changing the posts we then occupied. The general willingly assented to my proposition, but, in doing so, hinted that it was an almost impossible job, which, if lost, would probably cost me my life, but if gained would place us in a position to strike another effectual blow.

"After shaking hands with my brother officers, I bade good-by to General McClellan and his staff, and went rapidly to work preparing for the expedition. Dressing myself in a suit of heavy gray clothes, which was made up in the popular Southern style of tailoring, I left camp a little after midnight in company with one of the most successful scouts in the service, whose name was Parsons. Passing silently down through the camp, we quickly left the picket posts in the rear and in a minute more were standing on the river's bank, hidden from sight by a clump of bushes. Taking a general view of our whereabouts, we started, crawling on our hands and knees, to find a dug-out, which I had ordered to be placed in the afternoon near the bushes we were then in. Being unable to find it anywhere, Parsons said the only way left to us to get across dry-shod was to go down the stream two miles or so, where there was a ferry, and possibly we might get a boat of some kind.

"Taking a short cut through the woods, we soon reached the designated spot, but no boat was to be found. Seeing, however, the ferryboat moored to the opposite bank, I concluded at once what I would do, and in spite of Parsons' remonstrances and his assertion that signaling the scow would bring the rebs down on us in force, I determined to adopt a new plan, and stepping out on the bank gave three or four shrill whistles, which brought back an answer, 'Who's there?' Knowing the ferryman to be a rebel at heart, but professedly a patriot, I answered in a low but clear voice, giving the name of a well-known Confederate scout. A moment after I saw in the moonlight, which clearly defined the other shore, the ferryman let go his moorings, and in a few moments more the clumsy old scow was stemming her way across the stream and soon reached the bank at our feet.

"Having instructed Parsons in the game I was to play, I told him I would act as the general spokesman on the trip. As we were crossing to the other bank, I secured considerable knowledge of the rebels' line of defense from the boatman, who was quite communicative. The most important thing I learned was just what I had all the time expected, namely, that the opposite river bank was comparatively free from any large force of troops, Lee's command being posted several miles inland, while the only force within a distance of four miles was a squad of about 200 cavalry, who were patrolling the river bank for several miles on the lookout for spies and contrabands. He also told us that the headquarters of this detachment were a mile up the river. Not wishing to ask questions that would excite his suspicions, I turned the conversation to other subjects.

"On arriving at the ferry-house, I recollect that I looked at my watch and saw it was just 1 o'clock. An hour from camp, and two more before us in which to accomplish our design and get back to the stream. Hardly had we begun to pick our way through the dense undergrowth, revolver in hand, when Parsons, who was leading the van, heard the twigs snap in front of him, and, suddenly raising his weapon, brought it in line with a man's head. After a moment, during which time neither party made a motion, we heard a subdued voice whisper: 'Don't shoot, massa. Dis nigger giv up quick.' The anxiety of the black's speech told us that the pistol had been appreciated, and, with a half-suppressed chuckle, the scout lowered his pistol, and in a tone of authority began to question the man before him. Finding he could not, without force, elicit any information from him in that guise, I walked up, and, placing my hand on his shoulder, told him in a whisper who we were. The fellow immediately brightened up on learning that we were Yankees, and told us substantially the same story as had the boatman concerning the rebels' whereabouts.

"The negro being unable to direct us exactly to the location of the plantation, I concluded that we had now better separate, after arranging with Parsons where we would meet to recross the river in case we got through all right. I advised him to take a path which ran at right angles with a little lane, which I saw leading through the woods, thinking that if one did not lead to the house the other might. I then wished him good luck, and instructing him as to what information I wanted, started off alone over the other path, telling the negro he had better wait where he was until we returned. I had informed the scout, previous to starting, that if he had reasons to believe I was captured, to at once put for the river, and cross if he could to General McClellan with whatever information he might have secured. My walk down that lane was not as pleasant as it might have been, I assure you, and I was fully thirty minutes going about a mile.

"Suddenly I noticed that smoke was perceptible in the air, and in a moment more I came across the smoldering ruins of a camp-fire in the midst of a thick grove. Pursuing my way with care, I suddenly emerged from the grove and found myself on a closely-cut lawn to the right of a large, square, planter's mansion. The windows, unillumined by any interior light, glistened like silvery mirrors in the moonlight. I was quite surprised at first to run across my intended destination in such an unexpected quarter, but quickly gathering my faculties, I determined to get close up to the house on the left side, which was shaded completely from the moon, and there get as good an idea of the situation as possible, and then wait, like Micawber, for something to turn up. While accomplishing this I learned that there were only two sentries posted, one in the direct front of the house, the other far in the rear by the stables. Until I gained the desired shade I thought that the house was all asleep, but looking cautiously in a window, I saw through an open doorway in a further room a cavalry officer seated at a desk writing on what, from the distance, appeared to be an official report.

"Scarcely had I gazed on the scene a moment, when I heard the stillness of the night broken by the crack of a rifle in the distance, which was followed by a Southern yell for help. In a moment I was flat in the bushes, with a fiercely-beating heart and a strong belief that Parsons had got himself into trouble. Directly my fears were more than realized, as far as the trouble was concerned, for in another moment a second shout was heard, followed by the reports of several carbines, which created a general consternation in the house. The whole place was immediately swarming with soldiers. Just then I heard the colonel, whom I had seen writing, give the order, 'Every man out of this house and see what those shots mean.' Immediately the bugler sounded the 'to horse.'

"In leaving, the officer commanding ordered the two guards on duty 'to keep their posts and have an eye peeled for strangers,' and in less than two minutes more the last sound of the horses' feet had died away in the distance. Then, drawing a breath of relief, I arose and looked into the window and saw the papers lying just where the colonel had last placed them, he having in his hasty departure forgotten to put them away. I was just preparing to enter the window to get them when I saw the guard who had been stationed in the front enter the room. Going to the closet he took out a pocket flask, from which he drank deeply. Knowing every moment was precious, I abandoned my first plan of entering, and, running lightly around the house, passed through the front door. Advancing with a heavy cane in my hand, which I had picked up in the hall, I came face to face with the guard. Surprised at seeing me, he hesitated a moment, thinking I was an officer and had discovered his theft. Before he had time to utter a word, I brought the cane down on his head and he keeled over like a log.

"Hastily grasping some provisions and doing the papers up in a roll, I left the house, starting to return the way I came. I had not proceeded far, however, when I ran directly into a squad of four of the returning men. Knowing my case would be, as a spy, hopeless, if taken, I determined to sell out as dearly as possible, and therefore fired two shots from my revolvers, which I carried in my hands. Without waiting to see the result, I dashed into the dense undergrowth and started in a direction directly opposite to the one I had been previously pursuing, and over land where horsemen could not follow. Keeping up a steady run for half an hour, I left the remaining pursuers far behind. After going nearly ten miles further without knowing where I was, I concluded I would change the direction. After walking for half a mile or so in the bed of a small stream to elude the Confederates, should they put the dogs after me, I stopped before a rude hut standing by itself in the middle of a grove of maples, it being a cabin that was used only in sap times. Exhausted in body and mind, I threw myself on its rude floor of pine boughs and was soon fast asleep, dreaming of the pleasures I had not found while awake.

"How long I remained there I do not know, but when I arose the sun was shining brightly. Knowing the impossibility of an escape under the circumstances, I read the papers I had secured, making mental notes as I went along, and when done set them on fire and consumed the whole. Being nearly starved, I was obliged to seek some food, and after scraping my wits together, I determined to fix up as much as possible and look for some negro cabins. The inmates I knew would be willing to help a blue-coat across the lines, and it was absolutely necessary that the general should at once know what I had learned while on my hunt. I was suddenly brought to a standstill by the command, 'Halt!' and before I knew what had happened, I was on my way to a Confederate commander's headquarters to explain, if I could, why I was found so far from a town in so peculiar a condition.

"The story I told seemed to entirely satisfy the lieutenant commanding, but he said that orders were very strict, and that he should have to send me to Richmond, where I would be tried as a spy, and if convicted, hung, but if proved all right, safely returned to my home, which I said was in Baltimore. With this knowledge of my future career I was put under guard, but was well fed and permitted to go to sleep. At an early hour the next morning I was put in the hands of a detachment of military police, and with several others commenced the march to Richmond. Down the Shenandoah Valley we went, passing through land once smiling with plenty, but now, through the effects of the campaign, barren and as deserted as a beggar's pocket. After a long, tiresome march, we came in sight of the rebel stronghold, and as we passed up the streets, which were filled with men and women shouting at us and hurling the bitterest kind of execration on our heads, I felt an involuntary shudder pass over me. I then recognized for the first time the real danger I was in, being among the Union spies who were sent down for nominal trial, but really for execution. Fortunately for me, when we had left the commander's headquarters, the lieutenant, impressed with my asserted innocence, wrote a note to that effect to General Winder, into whose office I was then being ushered. On entering to write down the names of his prisoners, the officer in charge of us handed the note referred to to the general's clerks, the former being out for the day. Being in a great hurry, the letter was hastily perused and the clerk, turning to the prison guard, said that he guessed I was not a spy, but a pretty good candidate for Castle Thunder, and thereupon he tore up the letter and the written charges against me and I was sent to prison, but, by God's providence, not to the hangman's noose. Castle Thunder, which was a perfect 'hell on earth,' was now my home, and there I staid for weeks, starving in body and mind, until finally, after seven months' imprisonment, a successful tunneling expedition was entered upon and a dozen or more escaped, I among the number, but then a mere shadow of my former self.

"It would be too long a story for me to enter into the details of that dreadful flight. Tracked by bloodhounds, we were sometimes almost brought to bay, but a merciful hand seemed to protect us, and finally three of the twelve who escaped successfully eluded their pursuers. After traveling through the mountainous district of West Virginia for some weeks, we three then separated, for our commands were at different points, and hardly had I been left alone a day when I was again taken prisoner, but played off I was a Confederate, and to escape imprisonment finally joined the army, but, as you might know, in name only. After a while I got my reputation safely established, and one night successfully ran the picket-guard and brought up for the first time for nearly a year under the Stars and Stripes. I tell you it was a happy day for me.

"When the war finally ended I brought up in Galveston, Tex. Getting a start on the frontier as herdsman, a few weeks later, I went to the far Southwest, and as I grew into better circumstances established a ranch of my own. This I sold five years ago, and since that time have been located in Richmond, Va. As I did not know where any of my old army friends might be, and having no relatives here, I never wanted to come North until two or three months ago, when, spurred on by a sudden desire, I went to New York, and from there to Boston, and finally have brought up here in Portland, just twenty-three years after we started out, with buoyant hearts and brave determination."

The Confederate Grave Under the Roses.—The following touching incident is related by Mr. George F. Williams, in his "Bullet and Shell." (New York: Fords, Howard & Hulbert):

"Late in the afternoon of the first day of July we reached the picturesque town of Hanover. Near the cross-roads were lying the bloated carcasses of half a dozen cavalry horses, evidently slain in a brief skirmish between Pleasonton's and Stuart's troops, a few hours before our arrival.

" Close to the road, near the scene of the cavalry fight, stood a farmhouse, at the gate of which was an old-fashioned pump and horse-trough. The pump-handle was in constant motion, as the weary, foot-sore soldiers flocked around it to quench their thirst with the delicious water that flowed into the mossy trough.

" Coming up and waiting for my turn to drink, I noticed a sunburnt, gray-haired man leaning over his rude gate, watching the troops. He was dressed in a faded, well-worn suit of homespun, having, no doubt, spent the day in the hay-field; and I could see that he was pleased that his pump was doing such good service.

" 'Good evening, sir,' said I to him, removing my cap, and mopping the perspiration from my face. 'It's rather hot weather, this, for marching?'

" 'I 'spose 'tis, though I never did any marching,' was his brief response.

" As the old farmer uttered the words he moved a little, and my eye was attracted by a new-made grave among a clump of rose bushes, just inside the fence. Wondering at the sight, I ventured to ask the reason for its being there.

"' Whose grave is that?' said I, pointing to the mound of fresh earth.

"' A reb's,' he replied laconically. 'One that got killed in a fight the horsemen had here to-day.'

" 'Indeed! and so you buried him?'

"'Yes; buried him myself. They left him lyin' in the road out thar, just as he fell. I could do no less, you know.'

"'Of course! But why did you make your rose-garden a graveyard?'

"'Wa-al, it was the wimmen that wanted it so. Yer see, stranger,' and the old man's voice trembled and grew husky—'yer see, I had a boy once. He went out with the Pennsylvany Reserves, and fou't along with McClellan, down thar among them Chicka-oming swamps. And one day a letter come. It was writ by a woman; and she told us as how a battle had been fou't near her house, while she and another woman lay hid all day in the cellar. When the battle was o'er, them wimmen came out, and found our Johnny thar, his hair all bloody and tangled in the grass. So they digged a grave in the soft earth of their garden, and buried my boy right amongst their flowers, for the sake of the mother who would never see him again. So when I saw that poor reb a-layin' out thar, all dead and bloody in the dust of the road, I sed I'd bury him. And the gals, they sed, "Yes, father, bury him among the rose-trees." That's why I did it, stranger.'

"Then the poor old father's voice was choked by a smothered sob, while a faint cry behind him betrayed the presence of a sister to the dead hero lying in his garden grave near Richmond.

"'Indeed, sir,' said I, feeling my own throat tighten over the sweet pathos of the little story, 'I can appreciate the love you bear your dead son. It must be some consolation to remember what you have done for the man whose body lies there under the bushes.'

"'Yes, stranger; that 'ere grave ain't much,'—and the old man turned to look at the rude mound his hands had made—'it ain't much, but it will be something to remember our Johnny by.'

"Bidding the farmer good-by, I hastened after the regiment, my eyes dimmed with tears; but my spirits strangely strengthened by this touching instance of human love and forgiveness."

Humor of the Battlefield.—Many humorous incidents, says a writer in the *Century Magazine*, occurred on battlefields. A Confederate colonel ran ahead of his regiment at Malvern Hill, and, discovering that the men were not following him as closely as he wished, he uttered a fierce oath and exclaimed: "Come on! Do you want to live forever?" The appeal was irresistible, and many a poor fellow who had laughed at the colonel's queer exhortation laid down his life soon after.

A shell struck the wheel of a Federal fieldpiece toward the close of the engagement at Fair Oaks, shivering the spokes and dismantling the cannon. "Well, isn't it lucky that didn't happen before we used up all our ammunition," said one of the artillerists as he crawled from beneath the gun.

When General Pope was falling back before Lee's advance in the Virginia Valley, his own soldiers thought his bulletins and orders somewhat strained in their rhetoric. At one of the numerous running engagements that marked the disastrous campaign, a private in one of the Western regiments was mortally wounded by a shell. Seeing the man's condition, a chaplain knelt beside him, and, opening his Bible at random, read out Sampson's slaughter of the Philistines with the jawbone of an ass. He had not quite finished, when, as the story runs, the poor fellow interrupted the reading by saying: "Hold on, chaplain. Don't deceive a dying man. Isn't the name of John Pope signed to that?"

A column of troops was pushing forward over the long and winding road in Thoroughfare Gap to head off Lee after his retreat across the Potomac at the close of the Gettysburg campaign. Suddenly the signal officer who accompanied the general in command discovered that some of his men, posted on a high hill in the rear, were reporting the presence of a considerable body of Confederate troops on top of the bluffs to their right. A halt was at once sounded, and the leading brigade ordered forward to uncover the enemy's position. The regiments were soon scrambling up the steep incline, officers and men gallantly racing to see who could reach the crest first. A young lieutenant and some half dozen men gained the advance, but at the end of what they deemed a perilous climb they were thrown into convulsions of laughter at discovering that what the signal men took for Confederate troops were only a tolerably large flock of sheep. As the leaders in this forlorn hope rolled on the grass in a paroxysm of merriment they laughed all the louder at seeing the pale but determined faces of their comrades, who, of course, came up fully expecting a desperate hand-to-hand struggle. It is perhaps needless to say the brigade supped on mutton that evening.

As the army was crossing South Mountain the day before the battle of Antietam, General McClellan rode along the side of the moving column. Overtaking a favorite Zouave regiment, he exclaimed, with his natural *bonhommie :* "Well, and how is the Old Fifth this evening?" "First-rate, General," replied one of the Zouaves. "But we'd be better off if we weren't living so much on supposition." "Supposition?" said the General, in a puzzled tone. "What do you mean by that?" "It's easily explained, sir. You see we expected to get our rations yesterday; but as we didn't, we're living on the supposition that we did." "Ah, I understand; you shall have your rations, Zouzous, to-night," replied the General, putting spurs to his horse to escape the cheers of his regiment. And he kept his promise.

President Lincoln and the Soldiers —The soldiers who were bearing the heat and burden of the war always held a near place in Mr. Lincoln's heart and sympathy. Upon one occasion, when he had just written a pardon for a young soldier who had been condemned by court-martial to be shot for sleeping at his post as a sentinel, Mr. Lincoln remarked :

"I could not think of going into eternity with the blood of that poor young man on my skirts. It is not to be wondered at that a boy raised on a farm, probably in the habit of going to bed at dark, should, when required to watch, fall asleep ; and I cannot consent to shoot him for such an act." The Rev. Newman Hall, in his funeral sermon upon Mr. Lincoln, said that this young soldier was found dead on the field of Fredericksburg with Mr. Lincoln's photograph next to his heart, on which he had inscribed, "God bless President Lincoln."

At another time there were twenty-four deserters sentenced to be shot, and the warrants for their execution were sent to the President to be signed. He refused, and the general of the division went to Washington to see Mr. Lincoln. At the interview he said to the President that unless these men were made an example of, the army itself would be in danger. Mercy to the few is cruelty to the many. But Mr. Lincoln replied: "There are already too many weeping widows in the United States. For God's sake don't ask me to add to the number, for I won't do it."

On another occasion a young soldier had fallen out of ranks when his regiment passed through Washington, and, getting drunk, failed to join his regiment when it left the city. To the friend who came to secure a pardon, Mr. Lincoln said; "Well, I think the boy can do us more good above ground than under ground," and he wrote out the pardon.

In all such cases as the above, where the ordinary human weakness was the motive, Mr. Lincoln's heart was tender as a woman's, but to prove that he could entertain no sympathy for a cool, deliberate, mercenary crime, he was approached by the Hon. John B. Alley, of Massachusetts, one day, with a petition for the pardon of a man who had been convicted of engaging in the slave trade, and sentenced to five years' imprisonment and the payment of a fine of one thousand dollars. His term of imprisonment had expired, but in default of payment of the fine, he was still held. In answer to the appeal for pardon Mr. Lincoln said : "You know my weakness is to be, if possible, too easily moved by appeals for mercy, and if this man were guilty of the foulest murder that the arm of man could perpetrate, I might forgive him on such an appeal; but the man who would go to Africa and rob her of her children and sell them into an interminable bondage with no other motive than that which is furnished by dollars and cents, is so much worse than the most depraved murderer that he can never receive pardon at my hands. No, he may rot in jail before he shall have liberty by any act of mine."

Upon another occasion the wife of a rebel officer, held as a prisoner of war, begged for the relief of her husband, and to strengthen her appeal said that he was a very religious man. In granting the release of her husband, Mr. Lincoln said: "Tell your husband when you meet him that I am not much of a judge of religion, but that in my opinion the religion that sets men to rebel and fight against their government because they think that a overnment does not sufficiently help some men to eat their bread in the sweat of other men's faces, is not the sort of religion upon which men can get to heaven."

One day news of a great battle in progress reached Mr. Lincoln, and his anxiety was so great that he could eat nothing. Soon after he was seen to take a Bible and retire to his room, and in a few minutes he was overheard in one of the most earnest prayers for the success of our arms. Later in the day a Union victory was announced, and Mr. Lincoln, with a beaming face, exclaimed: "Good news! good news! The victory is ours, and God is good."

An Army Newsboy's Romance.—So many acts of heartlessness and cruelty during the great civil war have been recorded that it is a real pleasure to have an opportunity to record an act of manly kindness on the part of a gallant Confederate soldier to a Yankee boy. In the town of Bennington, in the Green Mountains of Vermont, in the spring of 1861, there lived a poor woman with six children, five boys and one little girl, the youngest of the former a stripling 14 years old. When the wires flashed the news from Washington all over our land that the rebels had fired upon the old flag at Fort Sumter, the four older boys responded to the country's call and hurried to the seat of war. The younger lad, his heart fired with genuine Green Mountain patriotism, ran away from home and, eluding pursuit, made his way to the camp on the Potomac. But his ardor was somewhat dampened by the discovery of the fact that he could not, in consequence of his youth and diminutiveness, enlist as a soldier. Determined to remain at the front, and having, as the saying is, to scratch for a living, he went to selling newspapers to the soldiers. Leaving the camp between New Baltimore and Warrenton about the 10th of November, 1862, he went to Washington for a supply of papers. Having accomplished his object, the young lad set out on horseback for the camp, having to travel a distance of thirty miles. A change of position by the army during his absence had occurred, and as a consequence he ran into the rebel picket line and was taken to General J. E. B. Stuart's headquarters, at a hotel in Warrenton, and from there sent to Libby Prison, in Richmond, arriving there November 13. Major Turner was in command of the prison, and when the young prisoner was brought into his presence, observing that he was a mere boy, the Major spoke kindly to him, and, after his name had been enrolled, asked him the customary question, if he had any money or valuables about his person. The frightened boy had managed to conceal his money, $380, in his boots, and in answer to the question, put his hand down, and while a tear-drop glistened in his bright eye and his boyish lip quivered, he brought it forth and handed it to the rebel major, and trying hard to choke down the swelling in his throat, he told of his widowed mother at home, his four brothers in the army, his having made his money selling papers, and saving it to send with his brothers' wages to his mother. The Major folded the boy's passes around the money and said to him : " You shall have this again, my boy, when you are permitted to go from here." Six weeks afterward the lad was paroled, and, repairing to Major Turner's office, the kind officer, handing him the package of money and the passes, just as he had received them, said: "Here is your money, my boy." With trembling hands, but a joyous heart, the little fellow took the package. He was sent to Washington, and a few weeks afterward was going his old rounds selling newspapers. The boy was Doc Aubrey, the newsboy of the Iron Brigade, who now resides in Milwaukee.

Building a Bridge in Seventeen Hours.—In July, 1861, General J. D. Cox's division was chasing General Henry A. Wise's Confederate forces up the Kanawha River, in West Virginia, and to impede the rapid advance of the Union troops the bridge across Pocotaligo Creek was destroyed. The stream was only a couple of rods wide, but its banks were steep and the bed of the creek was too much of a slough to allow fording by the wagon trains and artillery. The regular army engineers wanted a few weeks' time to prepare plans, and considered it necessary to send to Cincinnati for tools and material to construct a bridge. The General, being informed that the Eleventh Ohio Infantry Regiment, then encamped at "Poco," had a company composed entirely of mechanics, sent for the captain, and, after a short conference with that officer, directed him to put his men at work. Commencing at nine o'clock in the morning, in seventeen hours a substantial "bridge" was built across the creek, and which was used by army wagons, cannons and soldiers for a long time, probably until the war closed. A raft of logs, timbers from a deserted house, and poles cut in the woods near by, were the materials used for the bridge, the tools being a few axes and augers. These practical bridge-builders were members of Company K, principally machinists, molders, etc., from the shops of Lane & Bodley, of Cincinnati, the captain being their late employer, P. P. Lane, afterward colonel of the regiment

The Three Diamonds.—"Do you remember the diamonds we found up at old Gray Jake Wagner's house when we were making that little raid around Taylorsville?" was asked of Colonel Andrew M. Benson, of Portland, Me., by a former companion with whom he was dining at Syracuse, N. Y. The colonel at first failed to recall the circumstances, but on the mention of a certain Miss Wagner's name a relaxation of his features showed that all recollection of the episode was not lost, and the dinner party was soon in possession of the facts, as follows: In the latter part of the year 1864, Colonel Benson, the captain of the First District of Columbia cavalry, with Colonel James M. Gere, also captain at the time, Colonel Walpole, of Syracuse, and Lieutenant Correll, of Vermont, w're confined in the prison pen at Columbia, S. C., and during December they escaped and made their way to Crab Orchard, on Doe River Cove. There they found a company of 83 struggling Federal soldiers. Though in the heart of the enemy's country, the members of this little band were suddenly stimulated to excessive bravery by thus meeting with their fellows, and conceived it would be a fine joke to make a little raid on Taylorsville, a village nearly 50 miles further north. The daring of the scheme appeared when, upon examination, it was found that 30 of the men had just one round of ammunition, while 31 had only one extra charge. Six, however, were mounted, and, at the head of this plucky detachment of cavalry Captain Benson was placed. Captain Gere led the infantry, and the whole squad was in command of Lieutenant James Hartley. Such was the make-up of the band that started out with more pluck than powder to capture Taylorsville. About 40 miles of the distance had been covered when the plantation of a rebel was reached who was notorious in all the country round. A halt was ordered to treat with the owner, Gray Jake Wagner, who was at that time just walking out to feed his hogs.

"Oh, take what you want; but only spare my life," cried Gray Jake Wagner, throwing up his hands like a flash and dropping his pail of swill as a bullet whistled past his ear, advising him of his distinguished visitors.

"We want," said Captain Benson, "whatever you have of use to us." And it took but a glance to tell the astonished planter that nothing could come amiss to that ragged company so lately escaped from the horrors of a rebel prison. Now, among other members of the Wagner family was a pretty daughter of the old rebel, aged eighteen, who had just returned from boarding-school to spend the holidays. After listening to the conversation with her father, and catching a glimpse of the visitors, she ran frightened to her own room. The troops swarmed about the place like bees and rushed into the house at every door. Several soldiers soon found their way even to the room of the scared young lady and demanded the immediate surrender of her revolver and ammunition.

"I have no revolver," cried the frightened girl.

"You have," yelled one of the soldiers with an oath, "and you will give it up." But at just this juncture the tall form of Captain Benson, who was then a dashing officer of 28, appeared and he took in the situation at a glance. Drawing his revolver, he threatened to drop the first man who touched a thing in that room or failed to leave without a word. The men withdrew in silence, while the frightened Miss Wagner, with tears and sobs, expressed her heartfelt thanks to her gallant protector.

"What did you find in the house?" asked Captain Benson of the infantry officer, as they left the place. "I found these diamonds," he quietly added, pointing to three glistening teardrops on his shoulder. The raid did not extend very far beyond Gray Jake Wagner's. Taylorsville, they learned, was full of rebel soldiers, and the little party barely managed to reach the Union lines.

Miss Wagner obtained in some way the address of her benefactor, and afterward, by letter, it is said, she sent her thanks, which she could only partially express in the excitement of their meeting.

Night on the Field of Fredericksburg.—Twenty-two years have passed, writes General Chamberlain, of Maine, since "Fredericksburg." Of what then was, not much is left but memory. Faces and forms of men and things that then were have changed—perchance to dust. New life has covered some; the rest look but lingering farewells.

But, whatever changes may beautify those storm-swept and barren slopes, there is one character from which they can never pass. Death gardens, haunted by glorious hosts, they must abide. No bloom can there unfold which does not wear the rich token of the inheritance of heroic blood; no breeze be wafted that does not bear the breath of the immortal life there breathed away.

Of all that splendid but unavailing valor no one has told the story; nor can I. The pen has no wing to follow where that sacrifice and devotion sped their flight. But memory may rest down on some night scenes too quiet and sombre with shadow to be vividly depicted, and yet which have their interest from very contrast with the tangled and lurid lights of battle.

The desperate charge was over. We had not reached the enemy's fortifications, but only that fatal crest where we had seen five lines of battle mount but to be cut to earth as by a sword-swoop of fire. We had that costly honor which sometimes falls to the "reserve"—to go in when all is havoc and confusion, through storm and slaughter, to cover the broken and depleted ranks of comrades and take the battle from their hands. Thus we had replaced the gallant few still lingering on the crest, and received that withering fire which nothing could withstand by throwing ourselves flat in a slight hollow of ground within pistol shot of the enemy's works, and, mingled with the dead and dying that strewed the field, we returned the fire till it reddened into night, and at last fell away through darkness and silence.

But out of that silence from the battle's crash and roar rose new sounds more appalling still; rose or fell, you knew not which, or whether from the earth or air; a strange ventriloquism, of which you could not locate the source, a smothered moan that seemed to come from distances beyond reach of the natural sense, a wail so far and deep and wide, as if a thousand discords were flowing together into a keynote weird, unearthly, terrible to hear and bear, yet startling in its nearness; the writhing concord broken by cries for help, pierced by shrieks of paroxysm; some begging for a drop of water, some calling on God for pity; and some on friendly hands to finish what the enemy had so horribly begun; some with delirious, dreamy voices murmuring loved names, as if the dearest were bending over them; some gathering their last strength to fire a musket to call attention to them where they lay helpless and deserted; and underneath, all the time, the deep bass note from closed lips too hopeless or too heroic to articulate their agony.

Who could sleep, or who would? Our position was isolated and exposed. Officers must be on the alert with their command. But the human took the mastery of the official; sympathy of soldiership. Command could be devolved, but pity not. So with a staff officer I sallied forth to see what we could do where the helpers seemed so few. Taking some observations in order not to lose the bearing of our own position, we guided our steps by the most piteous of the cries. Our part was but little—to relieve a painful posture, to give a cooling draught to fevered lips, to compress a severed artery, as we had learned to do, though in bungling fashion ; to apply a rude bandage, which might yet prolong the life to saving ; to take a token or farewell message for some stricken home—it was but little, yet it was an endless task. We had moved to the right and rear of our own position—the part of the field immediately above the city. The farther we went the more need and the calls multipl'cd.

Numbers half-awakening from the lethargy of death or of despair by sounds of succor, begged us to take them quickly to a surgeon, and, when we could not do that, imploring us to do the next most merciful service and give them quick dispatch out of their misery. Right glad were we when, after midnight, the shadowy ambulances came gliding along and the kindly hospital stewards, with stretchers and soothing appliances, let us feel that we might return to our proper duty.

The night chill had now woven a misty veil over the field. Fortunately, a picket fence we had encountered in our charge from the town had compelled us to abandon our horses, and so had saved our lives on the crest ; but our overco had been strapped to the saddles, and we missed them now. Most of the men, however, had their overcoats or blankets—we were glad of that. Except the few sentries along the front, the men had fallen asleep—the living with the dead. At last, outwearied and depressed with the desolate scene, my own strength sank, and I moved two dead men a little and lay down between them, making a pillow of the breast of a third. The skirt of his overcoat drawn over my face helped also to shield me from the bleak winds. There was some comfort even in this companionship. But it was broken sleep. The deepening chill drove many forth to take the garments of those who could no longer need them, that they might keep themselves alive. More than once I was startled from my unrest by some one turning back the coat skirt from my face, peering, half vampire-like, to my fancy, through the darkness to discover if it, too, were of the silent and unresisting ; turning away more disconcerted at my living word than if a voice had spoken from the dead.

And now we are aware of other figures wandering, ghostlike, over the field. Some on errands like our own, drawn by compelling appeals; some seeking a comrade with uncertain steps amid the unknown, and ever and anon bending down to scan the pale visage closer, or, it may be, by the light of a brief match, whose blue, flickering flame could scarcely give the features a more recognizable or human look; some man desperately wounded, yet seeking with faltering step, before his fast ebbing blood shall have left him too weak to move, some quiet or sheltered spot out of sound of the terrible appeals he could neither answer nor endure, or out of reach of the raging battle coming with the morning; one creeping, yet scarcely moving, from one lifeless form to another, if, perchance, he might find a swallow of water in the canteen which still swung from the dead soldier's side; or another, as with just returning or last remaining consciousness, vainly striving to rise from a mangled heap, that he may not be buried with them while yet alive, or some man yet sound of body, but pacing feverishly his ground because in such a bivouac his spirit could not sleep. And so we picked our way back amid the stark, upturned faces of our little living line.

Having held our places all the night, we had to keep to them all the more closely the next day; for it would be certain death to attempt to move away. As it was, it was only by making breastworks and barricades of the dead men that covered the field that we saved any alive. We did what we could to take a record of these men. A Testament that had fallen from the breast pocket of the soldier who had been my pillow I sent soon after to his home—he was not of my command—and it proved to be the only clew his parents ever had of his fate.

The next midnight, after thirty-six hours of this harrowing work, we were bidden to withdraw into the town for refreshment and rest. But neither rest nor motion was to be thought of till we had paid fitting honor to our dead. We laid them on the spot where they had won, on the sheltered edge of the crest, and committed their noble forms to the earth, and their story to their country's keeping.

"We buried them darkly, at dead of night,
The sod with our bayonets turning."

Splinters of boards, torn by shot and shell from the fences we had crossed, served as headstones, each name hurriedly carved under brief match lights, anxiously hidden from the foe. It was a strange scene around that silent and shadowy sepulchre. "We will give them a starlight burial," it was said ; but heaven ordained a more sublime illumination. As we bore them in dark and sad procession, their own loved north took up the escort, and, lifting all her glorious lights, led the triumphal march over the bridge that spans the worlds—an aurora borealis of marvelous majesty ! Fiery lances and banners of blood and flame, columns of pearly light, garlands and wreaths of gold, all pointing upward and beckoning on. Who would not pass on as they did, dead for their country's life, and lighted to burial by the meteor splendors of their native sky ?

The Colonel's Foraged Breakfast.—Colonel Johnson, commanding the 108th Regiment, Illinois Volunteer Infantry, during the late war, up to the time he fairly earned and secured his "single star," was a strict disciplinarian. Straggling and foraging were especially tabooed by him ; certain and severe was the punishment of the culprit who was caught away from his command without authority, and if any foraged provisions were found on the scoundrel they were at once confiscated. As it was not practicable to return the provisions to the lawful owner, the colonel would have them served up at his own mess table, "to keep them from going to waste."

As a consequence, the colonel was cordially hated by many of his men, and many were the plans laid down by them "to get even" and circumvent him, but, owing to his astuteness, they generally came to grief.

One day a soldier of the regiment, who had the reputation of being "a first-class, single-handed forager," but who had nevertheless been repeatedly compelled to disgorge his irregularly procured supply of fresh meat, and as repeatedly to pass an interval of his valuable time in the regimental bull-pen, slipped away from camp and, after an absence of several hours, returned with a loaded haversack and tried to get to his tent without attracting any attention. He was noticed, however, and promptly arrested and escorted to regimental headquarters.

"Omar, you infernal scoundrel, you have been foraging again," said the colonel.

"No, I haven't."

"Haven't, eh! Let's see what is in your haversack. Leg o' mutton, eh! Killed some person's sheep," said the colonel. Omar was sent to the guard house as usual, and the foraged property to the colonel's cook.

The regimental mess, consisting of most of the field and staff officers, had fresh meat for supper and breakfast. During the latter meal the colonel happened to look out from under the tent fly that was in use as a mess-room, and noticed Omar, who was under guard cleaning up around headquarters, eyeing him very closely. The colonel remarked: "Well, prisoner, what is it?"

"Nothing, colonel," replied Omar, "except I was just wondering how you liked your breakfast of *fried dog.*"

Consternation seized the party at the table. With an exclamation or expletive, every one of them sprang to his feet, and from under the tent fly.

Omar ran for his life, and at once, as per preconcerted agreement, over half the men in the regiment commenced barking and howling like dogs—big dogs, little dogs, hoarse and fine, bass and soprano, fortissimo and mezzo-soprano, dogs 'round the corner and dogs under the house—in short, there was the "dog"-onedest kind of a racket made until the colonel grasped his sword, and, foaming with rage, rushed for the men's tents; but they were too old to be caught.

For a long time, though, they would "regulate" the colonel if he showed signs of being excessive by barking, but at their peril, for he would certainly have killed a *barker* if discovered.

After that breakfast the regimental mess strictly abstained from eating any second-hand foraged meat.

How Custer and Young Took Dinner.

Generals Pierce Young, of Georgia, and Custer were messmates and classmates and devoted friends at West Point. In the war they were major-generals of cavalry on opposing sides. One day General Young was invited to breakfast at the Hunter mansion in Virginia. The beautiful young ladies had prepared a smoking breakfast to which the general was addressing himself with ardor when a shell burst through the house. Glancing through a window, he saw Custer charging toward the house at the head of his staff. Out of the window Young went, calling to the young ladies, "Tell Custer I leave this breakfast for him." Custer enjoyed it heartily, and looked forward with pleasure to the dinner in the distance. In the meantime, Young, smarting over the loss of his breakfast and his hasty retreat, drove the Federal line back, and by dinner time was in sight of the Hunter mansion again. Custer, who was just sitting down to dinner, laughed and said: "That's Pierce Young coming back. I knew he wouldn't leave me here in peace. Here's my picture; give it to him, and tell him his old classmate leaves his love with his excellent dinner." And out of the window he went and away like a flash, while the Georgia general walked in and sat down to dinner.

The Noble Act of a Hero.

Louis Abear, says the Detroit *Free Press*, was a private in Company H, Fifth Michigan Cavalry, and made a good soldier. At the battle of Trevillian Station he was taken prisoner, and before his release he was confined in five different prison-pens and two jails.

While he was in Millen Prison, an exchange of sixty prisoners was to be made. The officer of the day told off sixty names at the door of the pen, but for some reason, probably because he was too ill, or perhaps dead, one man did not come forth. At that moment Louis, who had been sent out after fuel, under guard of course, came through the gates pushing a wheelbarrow loaded with wood.

"Here, Louis, here's a chance for you. We want sixty men to go North and are short one. Jump into the ranks here!" exclaimed the officer.

"To be exchanged?" asked Louis, trembling more than he did when under fire.

"Yes. Be quick."

"Then take Hank. He's sick, and will die if he remains here," and Louis darted into the hospital ward. Hank had a pair of pantaloons and shoes, but no coat or hat. Louis pulled off his, put them on Hank, and brought him out, weak and tottering. As Hank filed out the gate and once more breathed the air of freedom, Louis, hatless and coatless, took hold of the handles of his wheelbarrow and started for another load of wood.

Can mortal mind conceive of such an act? It cost him seven months of a living death, and all for a man with whom he was not even intimately acquainted.

And now for the other side of the picture. Ever since the close of the war, until a few months ago, when Hank died, these two men have lived right here in Wayne County, Hank with a home and family, Louis with neither; have met occasionally, but at no time did Hank ever refer to the act in Millen Prison that set him free and saved his life; never invited him to his home; never alluded to the past, or addressed his savior other than as a mere acquaintance. On his death-bed, however, he told the story, and asked his relatives, if they ever had an opportunity, to befriend Louis for his sake. It was tardy acknowledgment of one of the noblest acts the world has ever known.

The Confederate Spy.—In "Bullet and Shell," by George F. Williams (New York: Fords, Howard and Hulbert), we find the following interesting anecdote:

"I had just returned from an inspection of my line on the afternoon of the fourth day, having found everything provokingly quiet and uninteresting. The evening was deliciously cool, the breeze down the river being laden with the perfumes of the forest; and I experienced a fresh degree of pleasure in viewing the romantic scene after supper, carelessly lounging over the top of a boulder, smoking my pipe. My thoughts began drifting away again; and I had wholly forgotten my surroundings, when Dennis suddenly touched my arm, exclaiming:

" 'An' what the divil was that?'

" 'Confound you, corporal! what do you mean by startling me like that?' said I, angry at the unwonted interruption. 'What are you staring at, you idiot?'

" 'Why, I thought I saw a man down there on the other side,' he replied, not noticing my reproof, so intently was he peering across the river.

" 'It seems to me, Dennis, that you are always seeing somebody or something,' I retorted sarcastically. 'Hang it, man, be quiet! I see no one; and, if I did, he cannot eat us.'

" 'Troth, an' we wud be a tough mouthful. But, if ye didn't see him, Master Frank, I did. Yis; there he is now.'

" 'Where?' I whispered, now thoroughly aroused.

" 'Why, over there by that big birch-tree. There he is, sitting down on that flat bit of rock, for all the world like a big brown toad;' and Dennis pointed excitedly toward the upper end of the bend.

"Following the direction of Dennis' finger with my eyes, I saw that he was right. A man was there, sure enough, sitting among some rocks at the river's edge, as motionless as if made himself of stone.

" 'It must be one of the Confederate pickets,' said I; 'they are beginning to show themselves again. Tell Sergeant Foster I want him.'

"In a few minutes Sam was by my side.

" 'Sergeant, take your rifle, and pass along our line to the right. See that the men are on the lookout. There's a man down there on the opposite bank, and no doubt others above and below. Tell Sergeant Coulter to take the left and do the same.'

"The two sergeants disappeared on their respective errands, while I continued to watch the stranger, Dennis and the rest of my reserve scattering among the rocks for the same purpose. There was no need to enjoin silence, for all seemed to appreciate its necessity.

"The sun had gone down, but there was sufficient light left for us to discern the man crouching among the trees. I had noticed that he had no musket; and, as I watched him, I wondered what he intended to do, for it was now evident that his presence on the river had a definite purpose. Ten or fifteen minutes passed, yet the man made no sign or movement; and I was getting somewhat impatient, when he arose to his feet, and, turning round, dragged a log of wood from under the bushes, silently launching it into the water. As he did so, I saw that he had a revolver slung around his neck.

"'Begorra! he's going to cross,' whispered Dennis, over my head. 'Shall the b'yes give him a volley?'

"'No, no! Let him come, and we will capture him. Pass the word for no one to fire.'

"As I uttered the words the Confederate placed himself astride of the log and plunged boldly into the stream. It was evidently an old experience, for the fellow guided his log so adroitly that the current was carrying him straight toward our position. I saw that he intended to land among the driftwood under the rocks; so, hastily calling on three or four of the men nearest me, I crept down the bank to receive our visitor. By this time he had reached the middle of the river, coming swiftly toward us, evidently unconscious of the reception awaiting him. As he neared the pile of driftwood, the daring voyager shifted his right leg off the log, and, sitting sideways, made a sudden leap for the landing. So accurately had he judged his distance that, as he abandoned the log, he was able to scramble up among the loose chips and sticks forming the *débris*, soon rising to his feet.

"'Surrender, sir. You're my prisoner!' I exclaimed, as I rushed forward to seize the intruder.

"I was, however, too precipitate; for like a startled deer the Confederate turned before I could lay hands on him, and with a jeering laugh leaped lightly into the river.

"'Fire!' I shouted. At the same moment, I felt the mass of dry wood give way under my feet; and I fell into the water, hearing my men's muskets ring out a spattering volley as I took my involuntary bath. The current being so rapid, I believed I must swim for my life under the shower of bullets my men were sending after the fugitive; but the next instant my outstretched hand caught a friendly branch, so I was able to draw myself up to a safe footing. Scrambling over the rocks, I saw the Confederate reach the opposite bank in safety. As he reached the shore he waved his hand derisively, and then disappeared among the trees."

Some of Lincoln's Jokes.—President Lincoln has been made responsible for so many jokes, writes Ben: Perley Poore, that he reminds one of a noted Irish wit who, having been ruined by indorsing the notes of his friends, used to curse the day when he learned to write his name, as he had obtained such a reputation for willingness to oblige that he could not refuse. Mr. Lincoln might well have regretted ever having made a joke, for he was expected to say something funny on all occasions, and has been made answerable for all manner of jests, stories and repartee, as if he had combined all the elements of humor, commonplace heartlessness and coarseness, mingled with a passion for reviving the jokes of Joe Miller and the circus clowns. Yet he did say many excellent things. On one occasion Senator Wade came to him and said:

"I tell you, Mr. President, that unless a proposition for emancipation is adopted by the government, we will all go to the devil. At this very moment we are not over one mile from hell."

"Perhaps not," said Mr. Lincoln, "as I believe that is just about the distance from here to the Capitol, where you gentlemen are in session."

On one occasion, at a reception, when the crowd of citizens and soldiers were surging through the salons of the White House, evidently controlled by the somewhat brusque Western element, a gentleman said to him:

"Mr. President, you must diminish the number of your friends, or Congress must enlarge this edifice."

"Well," promptly replied Mr. Lincoln, "I have no idea of diminishing the number of my friends; but the only question with me now is whether it will be best to have the building stretched or split."

At one of these receptions, when a paymaster in full major's uniform was introduced, he said :

"Being here, Mr. Lincoln, I thought I would call and pay my respects."

"From the complaints made by the soldiers," responded the President, "I guess that is all any of you do pay."

Ward Lamon, when Lincoln had appointed him Marshal of the District of Columbia, accidentally found himself in a street fight, and, in restoring peace, he struck one of the belligerents with his fist, a weapon with which he was notoriously familiar. The blow was a harder one than Lamon intended, for the fellow was knocked senseless, taken up unconscious, and lay for some hours on the border of life and death. Lamon was alarmed, and the next morning reported the affair to the President.

"I am astonished at you, Ward," said Mr. Lincoln; "you ought to have known better. Hereafter, when you have to hit a man, use a club and not your fist."

Why the Teamster Broke His Promise.—In Holland's "Life of Lincoln" we find the following humorous anecdote, which is said to have amused the dead President exceedingly :

General Fisk, of Missouri, began his military life as a colonel ; and, when he raised his regiment in Missouri, he proposed to his men that he should do all the swearing of the regiment. They assented ; and for months no instance was known of the violation of the promise. The colonel had a teamster named John Todd, who, as roads were not always the best, had some difficulty in commanding his temper and his tongue. John happened to be driving a mule-team through a series of mud-holes a little worse than usual, when, unable to restrain himself any longer, he burst forth into a volley of energetic oaths. The colonel took notice of the offense, and brought John to an account. "John," said he, "didn't you promise to let me do all the swearing of the regiment?" "Yes, I did, colonel," he replied, "but the fact was the swearing had to be done then or not at all, and you weren't there to do it."

Heroic Sergeant Plunkett.—The death of Sergeant Thomas Plunkett, the armless hero of the Twenty-first Massachusetts Volunteers, which occurred at his home in Worcester, March 10, 1885, removes one of the most noted survivors of the civil war. In all of the many important battles in which his regiment, the Twenty-first Massachusetts, was engaged, Sergeant Plunkett distinguished himself by his gallantry. He was the hero of many incidents of individual intrepidity. After the battle of Chantilly Plunkett discovered that a favorite comrade was missing, and he started, unarmed, for the point where the regiment had first encountered the enemy, to search for his friend. He crept about cautiously for some time, when all at once he found himself facing an armed rebel. "You are my prisoner," exclaimed the Confederate. Plunkett hesitated a moment, not feeling sure as to the best course to pursue. He had no idea of surrendering, yet knew that it would be almost certain death if he attempted to run. He finally said:
"I think not," and at the same time sprang upon his enemy. Seizing him by the throat, he soon overpowered and disarmed him; then, presenting an imaginary pistol, he compelled the fellow to accompany him to our lines, where Plunkett delivered him up to General Reno.

But it was at the battle of Fredericksburg that Sergeant Plunkett performed the crowning act of heroism that gave him his fame and left him the "armless hero of Massachusetts." After repeated attempts had been made by the troops of the Second Corps to carry the enemy's works on Marye's Heights, during which regiment after regiment melted away before the fire of the strongly intrenched enemy, the Twenty-first Massachusetts, with the other regiments of Sturgis's division, was brought forward. In the charge men fell at every step, and by and by the colors went down, and with them Sergeant Collins, of Company A. Plunkett sprang forward and seized them. He then held them aloft and cried out to his comrades to follow him.

On pressed the Twenty-first, every man catching new inspiration from the conduct of the brave sergeant. The enemy redoubled their efforts, and shot and shell did frightful work among the little band of heroes. After a while, when the regiment had gained a point nearer the enemy's works than had been reached before, and while Sergeant Plunkett was waving the flag almost in the face of the foe and cheering on his comrades, a rebel shell burst beneath his feet, and the flag went down again; with it fell Plunkett.

When they tried to raise the flag again they found it lying beneath the poor fellow's body and wet with his blood. Both of his arms had been carried away by the explosion, and he had received other injuries. Soon after Sergeant Plunkett's heroic act became known to the State authorities, Adjutant-General Schouler suggested to Governor Andrew that the sergeant be commissioned. The Governor replied;

"No; it is better that he be known in history as Sergeant Plunkett."

A Confederate Scout's Story.—The following narrative is contributed to the Philadelphia *Times* by John S. Elliott, of Mobile, Ala., who during the civil war was a Confederate scout under General Wade Hampton:

"Soon after the investment of Petersburg, Va., by the Federal army under General Grant, in the summer of 1864, I was recalled from my field of operations in Northern Virginia and assigned to duty in the rear of the enemy's lines at Petersburg. I had before me quite an extensive territory, extending from the Petersburg & Weldon Railroad to the James River. It required some time to gain a knowledge of the country, its topography and people, before we could make our plans to the best advantage. Within a month the enemy had established his fortifications and had begun to scour the country outside his lines for the purpose of driving out all citizens who were unfriendly to the Union cause, and capturing and dispersing scouts and other soldiers who might venture outside the Confederate lines.

"There were several scouting parties, whose leaders were George D. Shadburn, Richard Hogan, Isaac Curtis, Ashby, Sanderson, myself and some others. We soon made it a hazardous business for the enemy to scout outside his lines with anything less than a hundred men well mounted and armed. Fight after fight took place between us and these small parties for more than a month. We often made an ambuscade, drawing the Federals into it and making a clean capture. Disputanta Station, on the Petersburg & Norfolk Railroad, was the scene and battle-ground of some of the most persistent hand-to-hand figh's. The enemy soon became more cautious and we became bolder and more daring, frequently going into the Federal lines and capturing the pickets as we came out.

"We had a telegraph operator who would cut the enemy's line and attach his wire so as to let the messages pass through his key, and in that way we got a number of important facts. These messages were being sent from the War Department in Washington City to General Grant, and from Grant and other generals to the department. One day while we were lying in the bushes listening to the clicking of our little key, a battle was going on south of Richmond, along the Nine Mile or Charles City road. Some general in command telegraphed to President Lincoln that he had stormed the enemy and captured two lines of breastworks, but the Confederates, reinforced, drove them back with heavy loss in killed and captured, and among the captured were Generals ———— and ————, whose names I have forgotten. The Federals soon found out that we were intercepting their messages, and they made it too warm for us to continue operations in that line.

"We went to work to break up scouting in neutral territory. There was an extensive district of country, interspersed with creeks, swamps and woods. The population was devoted to the cause of the South and that gave us great advantages. On one occasion I applied to General Hampton for forty well-mounted and armed men to attack and defeat one of these persistent and adventurous patrol parties that had given us a good deal of trouble. They came up with us at times, and greatly outnumbering us, we had to resort to flight to avoid being killed or captured. They boasted to the citizens that they intended to have us, dead or alive, if we staid in that country, and the sooner we left the better. The men asked for were furnished.

"We hauled down about a half mile of telegraph wire along the Petérsburg and Weldon Railroad late in the evening, rolled it into small bundles and carried it six or eight miles, and during the night formed an ambush. We stretched the wire across the road just high enough to catch a man above the saddle and wound it around trees to secure it. This was done at the head of a long cut in the road, and extending it more than a hundred yards back on each side and securing it by wrapping it around the trees, we made the wire very much like a partridge net. If we could get the enemy's cavalry into it we intended to charge down on the troopers and the wire in front would sweep the rider off and let the horse go, which would so excite and confuse them that we could capture them without much fighting.

"During the night some of my men, while scouting along the enemy's picket line, met with Ashby and told him where I was and what I intended to do the next day. He gathered several of his party and just before day he joined us. I was very glad to see him and to have his aid. I had been with him in fights and adventures that tried men's courage, and knew that there was not a braver or more gallant soldier in General Lee's army. I requested him to take charge of the head of our ambuscade and I would take the rear end, where the fight would begin. Our plan was that every man was to remain hidden until I opened the fight, and then all the men were to rush to the front and capture those nearest to them, and in that way we would secure all who got into our net. The next day was Sunday, a bright and beautiful morning. We were on the lookout at an early hour, with vedettes posted some distance out with signals of the enemy's approach. Hour after hour wore away without any sign of their coming. Toward noon two or three scouts from Shadburn's party, who had heard of our intended attack, joined us. They had come from the direction we expected the enemy and saw nothing that indicated a Yankee scout that day. We had begun to despair of any chance that day when one of the vedettes came running in and reported the enemy coming in our direction in strong force.

"I immediately went to an elevated point near by, and with

my spy-glass could see quite a column of cavalry riding toward us at a leisurely gait. I returned and told the boys to get into their blinds and lay low until I opened the fight, and then come out and show their hands. On the enemy came, as unconscious as if there was no war. The advance guard of about six men passed into our net laughing and talking, and of course never had the least idea that a deadly snare was set for them in that thick woods on both sides of the road. In a few moments the head of the column came into the snare also. As soon as we got as many as I thought we could manage, I sprang from my hiding place to within ten feet of the head of the column, fired a pistol over their heads and halloed 'Charge!' The Federal column broke in an instant, the rear half flying for dear life. We closed in upon the others, and such a scramble was rarely seen during the entire war.

"The men came out of their blinds promptly and in fine order, shouting at the top of their powerful voices, 'Surrender! Surrender!' and at the same time firing their guns over the heads of the already terrified enemy. The enemy made a grand rush and discovered—as some of the prisoners afterward said—that they were in a wire net and thought that we intended to murder them. They went with such force against the wire that it broke and most of them escaped. The first man who struck it was killed and a number of others were badly hurt, all of whom fell into our hands. In their extreme fright quite a number jumped off of their horses and ran through the woods toward their lines. Many of the horses became riderless and in the excitement ran after their dismounted owners."

Mutiny in Time of War.—It was in September, 1861. The old Fourth Connecticut infantry lay at White Oak Springs, a few miles from Frederick City, Maryland. The regiment was ragged, nearly barefooted, with no pay, and generally discontented and demoralized. There was a doubt in the minds of the men as to whether the United States had accepted them or whether they were still in the service of the State of Connecticut: the general government had neither paid nor clothed them, and the State uniforms which they wore when they left Hartford in May had become unfit for service; there was not a whole pair of trousers in the regiment, and the old green felt blankets were utilized by many as a covering by day as well as by night. Some of the men thought that the regiment ought to go home; that they were out only for three months, and an effort was being made to keep them for three years. The fact was, the regiment was mustered in for three years, but there were men who did not quite understand it, and so the trouble grew; and one morning Captain Lepprell, of Company K, reported to headquarters that his company were standing in the company street with their rifles in their hands, but absolutely refusing to obey his orders.

Lieutenant-Colonel White went over to Company K street, and there stood the men in line, their rifles at order arms, their cartridge boxes on, forty rounds of ball cartridge in each man's box, and their rifles, perhaps, loaded. Colonel White tried his authority, but the men ignored him; oaths and mutterings of discontent were heard from all along the line. Colonel White returned to headquarters satisfied that the authorities had got to deal with an armed and stubborn mutiny.

Captain Kellogg, of Company B, was ordered to get his company into line. "Company B, fall in," was the order next heard, and in a brief space of time Captain Kellogg reported his men in line. Lieutenant-Colonel White then came before Company B and made them a short address, at the close of which he said: "Now, men, you will have an opportunity to show your subordination or insubordination. Any of you men who are not willing and ready to obey any and all orders given by your officers can step two paces to the front." Not a man moved. Captain Kellogg then took command of the company and they were marched over to Company K street, and halted directly in front of, and about five paces from, Company K, facing them. The situation then was about as follows:

Company K armed with muzzle-loading rifles, not known to the authorities whether loaded or not, the men standing at order arms and having in their cartridge boxes forty rounds of ball cartridge each, and every man stubborn and insubordinate.

Company B, standing at "shoulder arms," armed with Sharp's breech-loading rifles, not loaded, each man with forty rounds of ball cartridge in his cartridge box, and every man subordinate and awaiting orders.

Captain Lepprell, of K Company, then gave the order to his company, "Shoulder arms." Not a man responded to the order; but oaths and threats were heard along the line. Captain Kellogg then assumed command of K Company, and ordered, "Shoulder arms!" Not a man responded. Turning to Company B, Captain Kellogg ordered, "Load for action," and every rifle came down to the position of load, the chamber was thrown open with a click, ball cartridge was inserted in each rifle, the chamber closed, the hammer thrown back to half cock and the next order awaited. It came, "B Company, ready!" and every hammer went up to full-cock.

"Aim!" and every man in Company B looked along his rifle barrel into the very face of his comrade in Company K.

Turning to Company K, Captain Kellogg ordered, "K Company, shoulder arms." Not a man responded.

Drawing out his watch, Captain Kellogg said: "If that order is not obeyed in sixty seconds, there will be no Company K in this regiment;" and every man in both companies knew he meant just what he said.

Thirty seconds passed, and no one in Company K had weakened. It was a thrilling moment; but ere the second hand marked forty-five seconds, the muskets of Company K began to come to a shoulder, and in less than ten seconds more, every man stood at "shoulder arms." The welcome order to B Company was, "Recover arms." If any man has stood at "aim" for a minute, he will know how welcome the order was; but if he has stood at "aim" against his own comrades for a minute, he will know how more than welcome the order "Recover arms" was to Company B.

The next order was to Company K, "Order arms." Every man responded promptly. "Stack arms," and every rifle was stacked instantly. "Two paces to the rear; march," and Company K were disarmed. Company B were ordered to shoulder arms, and were then marched in between Company K and their rifles. Company K were then marched as prisoners to headquarters, where each man's arms were bound with ropes and the whole company were taken off under guard to General Banks' headquarters and turned over to the provost marshal. After several weeks of confinement they were all returned to duty, and in less than six months the old Fourth Connecticut Infantry was transformed into the First Connecticut Heavy Artillery, and had become the best drilled, disciplined, clothed, armed and accoutred regiment in the volunteer service. In *morale, esprit de corps*, physique and all characteristics that make up a splendid regiment, it stood in the front rank, and from that time to the end of the war it did most excellent service, winning numerous emblazonries for its colors. Captain Kellogg was afterward promoted to the colonelcy of the Second Connecticut Heavy Artillery, and fell dead pierced with many bullets while leading his regiment in a gallant charge at Cold Harbor.

Stonewall Jackson's Bridge-Builder.—A useful man to Stonewall Jackson was old Miles, the Virginia bridge-builder. The bridges were swept away so often by floods or burned by the enemy that Miles was as necessary to the Confederate army as Jackson himself. One day the Union troops had retreated, and burned a bridge across the Shenandoah. Jackson, determined to follow them, summoned Miles.

"You must put all your men on that bridge," said he; "they must work all night, and the bridge must be completed by daylight. My engineer will furnish you with the plan, and you can go right ahead."

Early next morning Jackson, in a very doubtful frame of mind, met the old bridge-builder.

"Well," said the general, "did the engineer give you the plan for the bridge?"

"General," returned Miles slowly, "the bridge is done. I don't know whether the pictur' is or not."

From that time forth General Jackson allowed Miles to build the bridges after his own fashion, without annoying him with "pictur's."

A Woman's Courage at Gettysburg.—Mrs. Peter Thorn, of Gettysburg, lived in the house at the entrance of the borough cemetery. The house was used as headquarters by General O. O Howard. Mrs. Thorn's husband was away from home at that time (serving in the 148th regiment of Pennsylvania volunteers, and stationed in Virginia), leaving her with two quite young children. During the first day of the fight General Howard wanted some one to show him and tell about different roads leading from Gettysburg, and asked a number of men and boys who were in the cellar of the house to go with him and point them out. But these persons were all fearful and refused to go. Then Mrs. Thorn showed her courage and patriotism by voluntarily offering to show the roads. This offer was at first refused by General Howard, who said he did not wish a woman to do what a man had not the courage to do. Mrs. Thorn persisted in her offer, saying: "Somebody must show you, and I can do it; I was born and brought up here, and know the roads as well as anybody." Her offer was accepted, and with the general and his horse between her and the fire of the enemy, Mrs. Thorn went from one spot to another pointing out the different roads. When passing along the line of troops the general was greeted with: "Why do you take a woman for a guide? This is no place for her." "I know it," said the officer, "but I could not get a man to come; they were all afraid." This answer to them started cheers for Mrs. Thorn, which lasted several minutes and showed that our soldiers admired the courage shown at such a time.

Lincoln's Terrible Anxieties.—During these long days of terrible slaughter the face of the President was grave and anxious, and he looked like one who had lost the dearest member of his own family. I recall one evening late in May, when I met the President in his carriage driving slowly toward the Soldiers' Home. He had just parted from one of those long lines of ambulances. The sun was sinking behind the desolate and deserted hills of Virginia; the flags from the forts, hospitals and camps drooped sadly. Arlington, with its white colonnade, looked like what it was—a hospital. Far down the Potomac, toward Mount Vernon, the haze of the evening was gathering over the landscape, and when I met the President his attitude and expression spoke the deepest sadness. He paused as we met, and, pointing his hand toward the wounded men, he said : "Look yonder at those poor fellows. I cannot bear it. This suffering, this loss of life is dreadful." Recalling a letter he had written years before to a suffering friend, whose grief he had sought to console, I reminded him of the incident, and asked him : "Do you remember writing to your sorrowing friend these words : 'And this, too, shall pass away. Never fear. Victory will come?'" "Yes," replied he, "victory will come, but it comes slowly."

His friends and his family, and especially Mrs. Lincoln, watched his careworn and anxious face with the greatest solicitude. She and they sometimes took him from his labors almost in spite of himself. He walked and rode about Washington and its picturesque surroundings. He visited the hospitals, and, with his friends, and in conversation and visits to the theatre, he sought to divert his mind from the pressure upon it. He often rode with Secretary Seward, with Senator Sumner and others. But his greatest relief was when he was visited by his old Illinois friends, and for a while, by anecdotes and reminiscences of the past, his mind was beguiled from the constant strain upon it. These old friends were sometimes shocked with the change in his appearance. They had known him at his home, and at the courts in Illinois, with a frame of iron and nerves of steel ; as a man who hardly knew what illness was, ever genial and sparkling with frolic and fun, nearly always cheery and bright. Now, as the months of the war went on, they saw the wrinkles in his face and forehead deepen slowly into furrows, the laugh of old days was less frequent, and it did not seem to come from the heart. Anxiety, responsibility, care, thought, disasters, defeats, the injustice of friends, wore upon his giant frame, and his nerves of steel became at times irritable. He said one day, with a pathos which language cannot describe: " I feel as though I shall never be glad any more." During these four years he had no respite, no holidays. When others fled away from the heat and dust of the capital, he remained. He would not leave the helm until all danger was passed and the good ship of state had weathered the storm.—*Arnold's Life of Lincoln.*

A Brave Irish Soldier.—The Army of the Potomac, says a writers in *Peck's Sun*, contained no braver or better soldier, no kinder or more pleasant comrade, than genial Ed Leahy, of Company I, Twelfth New York Volunteers. As a forager he was the coolest, most audacious and ready-witted man I ever knew, unless, indeed, I except another Irishman of the same company, named Tim Dwyer.

When McClellan began his celebrated "change of base" which, after seven consecutive days of hard marching and terrible fighting, resulted in the placing of his shattered and exhausted army safe under the guns of our gunboats at Harrison's Landing, on the James River, Leahy, with others of our company, was detailed to guard the "grapevine telegraph" not far from Gaines' Mill.

In the confusion which followed the day's fighting at Mechanicsville, and the retreat from that place, this detail was never relieved or withdrawn, and when, on that disastrous second day of the seven days' fighting, the Fifth Corps, under Porter, was defeated at Gaines' Mill and retreated across the Chickahominy, Stuart's rebel cavalry, sweeping around what had been our right and rear, found them still at their post, where Leahy, who was the non-com. in charge, had persisted in staying until relieved, although they could plainly hear the roar of the progressing battle, and knew that if not soon relieved by our own men they would be by the rebels. Consequently they were not much surprised when, just before night, they found themselves surrounded by the rebel cavalry, and, after firing a few shots, were compelled to surrender.

When called upon to give up their arms, the first to do so was a man named Hitchcock, better known in his company as "Bowels," and as he handed up his gun to one of the rebels he tremblingly said, "You can see that my gun is perfectly clean. I have not fired a shot at you."

"I have, then," quoth indignant Ed as he swung his gun around his head and smashed off the stock against an apple tree, "as many as I could. And if you want my gun there it is, and much good may it do you."

"That's our sort, Yank," answered the cavalryman who had been waiting with outstretched hands to receive the gun. "We hate a coward and I reckon you'll get none the worse treatment among us because you show the true grit. Now fall in right smart and git."

And in five minutes the boys were on their way to long weeks of suffering in the prisons of Libby and Belle Island.

During the time that Leahy was a prisoner on Belle Island, the Confederates were very indignant because persons in the North struck off large quantities of *fac-similes* of their paper money. They considered it an insult to the confederacy that an imitation, a "counterfeit" of their "legal tender," was in the hands of our children as playthings and curiosities. And when it was learned that our boys in the army were passing large quantities of it on the unsuspecting Southerners for genuine Confederate money, there was a perfect howl of rage, and President Davis issued a proclamation, making it a hanging offense if any of our men were convicted of passing the obnoxious imitation.

Leahy had in some way procured a five-dollar note of this description, and being destitute of other money, he one day purchased with it a watermelon from a vender who had been passed inside the guard.

The melon was a luxury not often obtainable there, and, while the boys were eating it, they congratulated Ed on his having so nicely fooled the melon peddler, though all agreed it might prove a sorry joke after all, if he were found out.

Not many hours had elapsed before it was whispered to Ed that a sergeant and squad of men were searching for the man who had bought a melon with a *fac-simile* Confederate note.

"Bedad," said Ed, assuming for the occasion a strong brogue, "and I'm the lad that'll be after helping to find 'im."

And, after hastily exchanging his blouse with one of the boys for a cavalryman's jacket, he coolly walked up to the sergeant and said, "Is it the man pwhat bo't the melon ye'd be after spakin' wid?"

"Yes," said the sergeant. "Do you know him?"

"Know him, is it? And I just after ating a big pace of that same? An' the tashte of it still in me mouth? Begorra, I'd be after knowin' him forninst any b'y in this bastely hole The fine dacent lad that he is."

"All right, my man," said the sergeant. "You just walk around with me and point him out, and I will give you a dollar."

"Throth," said Ed, "an' I'm the b'y that'll do that same," and after a long and diligent search, during which Ed several times pretended to have discovered him, only to discover, on closer inspection, that he was mistaken, he finally decided that he was not to be found, and wound up his complaint at not being able to earn the dollar by asking the sergeant, "An' phwat would yez be after wantin' wid the laddie buck? Is it a furlough ye'd be after givin' 'im?"

"Yes," said the sergeant. "A d——d long one. We meant to *hang him* for passing counterfeit money, and we will, too, if we find him."

"Howly mither o' Moses," said Ed, as he lifted up his hands in horror not altogether assumed, for he had all the time been aware of his probable fate if found out. "An' is it *that* yez wanted wid 'im? May the divil fly away wid me if I aint plazed that ye didn't find 'im thin. An' be the powers, I hope yez never will."

And they did not, for the boys all admired Ed's cool courage and kept the secret well. He was soon after exchanged, and came safely back to us not long after the battle of Antietam.

How Sheridan's Ride Looked to a Spectator.—The following account of how "Sheridan's Ride" looked to a spectator at one end of it, writes General James Comley, was copied by Mr. Whitelaw Reid from my private diary lent him for "Ohio in the War," and I know it is true : "Crook was lying a rod or two to our left. Hayes and I were together with our commands. He was badly bruised by his fall when his horse was killed under him, and had several slight wounds beside. He was teasing me and grumbling because we did not advance, instead of waiting for the enemy.

"Suddenly there is a dust in the rear, on the Winchester road, and almost before we are aware, a fiery-looking, impetuous, dashing young man in full major-general's uniform, and riding furiously a magnificent black horse, literally flecked with foam, and no poetic license about it, reins up and springs off by General Crook's side. There is a perfect roar as everybody recognizes Sheridan. He talks with Crook a little while, cutting away at the tops of the weeds with his riding-whip. General Crook speaks half-a-dozen sentences that sound a great deal like the whip, and by that time some of the staff are up. They are sent flying in different directions. Sheridan and Crook lie down and seem to be talking, and all is quiet again except the vicious shells of the different batteries and the roar of artillery along the line. After awhile Colonel [James W.] Forsyth comes down to our front and shouts to the General, "The Nineteenth Corps is closed up, sir.' Sheridan jumps up, gives one more cut with his whip, whirls himself around once, jumps on his horse and starts up the line. Just as he starts he says to our men: 'We are going to have a good thing on them now, boys!' It don't sound like Cicero or Daniel Webster, but it doubled the force at our end of the line. [I may say now, that it don't sound even like Buchanan Read.]

"And so he rode off, a long wave of yells rolling up to the right with him. We took our posts, the line moved forward— and the balance of the day is already history."

I suppose there is no necessity for burdening you with a description of our part in the advance, as there is no dispute as to our being there, or as to our place in the line. One incident may be of interest. At one of the pauses in this forward movement our company was delayed by a very high rail fence I (can hardly believe such a fence was left, but it was). Crook was on his horse, and had passed the fence when Hayes climbed up, and, by holding to one of the "stakes" and standing on the "rider," was more elevated than Crook, and could use his glass more effectively. He was able then to give Crook some important information, which I did not hear. But the result was that Hayes mounted his horse and dashed to the front at a headlong gallop, ahead of his infantry. I have learned since that he found Captain Dupont, who was moving down the pike, and under his immediate orders Captain Dupont passed through Middletown at a swinging trot, with his own battery, going to the front. Hayes, being very well mounted, and free to "cut across," got ahead out of sight, and on the eminence near where our camps had been, found General Sheridan entirely alone, using his glass in the most excited manner.

As soon as he saw Hayes he yelled at him: "If I had a battery here we could knock —— out of their train and capture all their artillery?" Hayes answered: "All right, general; I've got just what you want, coming as fast as it can!" He galloped back to Dupont, who immediately started all his horses at a gallop, and came down the pike like a whirlwind. The first shell he fired lit in the very midst of a narrow place where the head of the enemy's retreating column had got gorged by attempting to pass too many abreast. General Hayes has described the scene to me vividly, and it is enough to make one get up and give three cheers all alone by himself to think of it as he describes it—shell after shell dropping in the thickest of the throng, drivers cutting traces and scampering out of it, teams, ammunition, caissons and cannons abandoned and left literally piled up by the gorge.

Admiral Porter's Tribute to Grant.—The following extract is from a work entitled "Anecdotes and Reminiscences of the Civil War," by Admiral Porter:

In the history of the world's sieges nothing will be found where more patience was developed, more endurance under privations or more courage shown than by the Union forces at the siege of Vicksburg, while on the part of the besieged it was marked by their great fertility of resource in checking almost every movement of ours, and for the long months of suffering and hardship they underwent.

It belongs of right to General Grant to tell the story of that event, for in no case during the war did he so clearly show his title to be called a great general, nor did he elsewhere so fully exhibit all the qualities which proved him to be a great soldier.

If General Grant had never performed any other military act during the war, the capture of Vicksburg alone, with all the circumstances attending the siege, would have entitled him to the highest renown. He had an enemy to deal with of twice his force, and protected by defenses never surpassed in the art of war.

I saw, myself, the great strongholds at Sebastopol of the Malakoff tower and the Redan, the day after they were taken by a combined army of 120,000 men; and these strongholds, which have become famous in ballads and story, never in any way compared with the defenses of Vicksburg, which looked as if a thousand Titans had been put to work to make these heights unassailable.

I am told there were fifty-six miles of intrenchments thrown up, one within the other.

The hills above, with their granite rocks standing in defiance, were enough to deter a foe without having intrenchments bristling with cannon and manned by the hardiest troops in the Confederacy.

After it was all over and General Grant could see the conquered city lying at his feet, he could well afford to laugh at his vile traducers, who were doing all they could to hamper him by sending telegrams to the seat of government questioning his fitness for so important a command.

If those who lent themselves to such things could be followed through the war, it would be found that they never made a mark, put them where you would; nor did they achieve any good for the government.

That was a happy Fourth of July when the Confederate flag came down at Vicksburg and the Stars and Stripes went up in its place, while Meade's force at Gettysburg was driving Lee's army back to Richmond tattered and torn.

That day, so glorious in the annals of our history, lost nothing by the two brilliant events which were added to our fame and made it still more dear in the heart of every American.

When the American flag was hoisted on the ramparts of Vicksburg my flagship and every vessel of the fleet steamed up or down to the levee before the city.

We discerned a dust in the distance, and in a few moments General Grant, at the head of nearly all his generals, with their staffs, rode up to the gangway and, dismounting, came on board. That was a happy meeting, with great handshaking and general congratulation.

I opened all my wine lockers, which contained only Catawba on this occasion. It disappeared down the parched throats which had tasted nothing for some time but bad water. Yet it exhilarated that crowd as weak wine never did before.

There was one man there who preserved the same quiet demeanor he always bore, whether in adversity or victory, and that was General Grant.

No one, to see him sitting there with that calm exterior amid all the jollity, and without any staff, would ever have taken him for the great general who had accomplished one of the most stupendous military feats on record.

There was a quiet satisfaction in his face that could not be concealed, but he behaved on that occasion as if nothing of importance had occurred.

General Grant was the only one in that assemblage who did not touch the simple wine offered him; he contented himself with a cigar; and let me say here that this was his habit during all the time he commanded before Vicksburg, also while he commanded before Richmond, though the same detractors who made false representations of him in military matters before Vicksburg misrepresented him also in the matter above alluded to.

The Last Gasp of Lee's Army.—General Sheridan tells a very interesting story about the last campaign against Lee, and the incidents of the surrender. It will be remembered that he headed off Lee at Appomattox Court House, and captured eleven trains of supplies which were waiting for him there. When Lee found out that he had no stores or ammunition for his army, and that his retreat was cut off, he sent a flag of truce, which Custer received and conducted to Sheridan. The two armies lay on their arms waiting for Grant, who was on his way to the front.

In the meantime Sheridan and some of his staff started to ride over toward Appomattox Court House, when they were fired upon by a regiment of rebels half concealed among some underbrush. The General and his party waved their hats toward the place where the shots came from, and made all sorts of demonstrations to silence the unexpected and mysterious attack, but to no purpose. Finally the Confederate officer who brought the flag and Major Allen, of Sheridan's staff, rode over to see what the matter was.

They found a South Carolina regiment, whose colonel, in a grandiloquent tone, informed them that the war wasn't over, and that he and his regiment did not recognize the authority of General Lee to make terms for peace. "Be Gawd, sir," exclaimed this gallant Johnny, "South Carolinians never surrender!"

The two officers rode back to General Sheridan, who, with his party, had retired under cover, and reported to him the situation. The general called Custer, and told him there was one regiment over in the brush which hadn't got enough of it, and it would be well for him to go over there and "snuff it out." Custer ordered his bugler to sound "forward," and, at the head of a regiment, dashed across the interval which lay between the two armies, which were drawn up in long lines and stood at rest. It was a beautiful Sunday morning—a perfect spring day—and the sight of that regiment, with Custer's long, tawny hair as their banner, dashing at full gallop across the fields, evoked a cheer from both armies.

Meantime Sheridan had reached the court house, where he met General Gordon, recently Senator from Georgia, and General Wilcox, who had been his classmate at West Point, but whom he had not seen for many years. Wilcox has since been Doorkeeper of the United States Senate.

While this party were sitting on the steps of the court house, chatting familiarly over the situation. heavy musketry was heard in the distance. Gordon looked up in anxiety and alarm, and asked one of his aids to ride over in that direction and find out what it meant. "Never you mind, General," said Sheridan. "It's all right. I know what it means. Custer is over there having some fun with a South Carolinian who never surrenders." Gordon insisted upon sending the officer to stop the fight, but before he got there the doughty colonel had presented Custer with a very much battered sword. It was the last gasp of the Army of Northern Virginia.

A Rocket Battery.—The following incident is related by Colonel E. Z. C. Judson ("Ned Buntline"):

In the winter of 1863 an infantry brigade, with Howard's Battery L, Third Artillery, and two battalions of cavalry, the Eleventh Pennsylvania and First New York Mounted Rifles, all under General Wessels, made a reconnoissance out from Suffolk, Va., on the Franklin road.

The mud was hub deep to the gun carriages, and they had to double teams to get the guns along at all. The infantry spreading through the fields off the roads got along a little better; but it was hard marching and growlers were in the majority. About ten or twelve miles out the cavalry drove into a rebel picket ahead of us, and soon after we were checked by a heavy battle line of the men in gray.

The brigade was at once deployed and skirmishers were thrown out to feel the enemy while we waited for the guns to come up. They were far in the rear and there was no telling when they could be got to the front.

Suddenly from a little knoll in front of the rebel position a rocket battery, a recent importation on an English blockade-runner, opened sharp upon us. The huge rockets tearing and hissing through the trees and underbrush scared the cavalry horses fearfully, and the men were scared about as badly. Not one in a hundred of them had ever seen a rocket, except such as are used in fireworks, and the horrible missiles appeared worse than they really were.

The writer had seen Congreve rockets used to repel a Seminole attack on Fort Dallas, near Key Biscayno, in 1839, and probably he was about the only one in the command who knew what such a battery could do. General Wessels was furious We could only reply to the rockets with musketry. A deep stream and a muddy flat ahead of us made a cavalry charge next to impossible, and the infernal rockets were literally demoralizing the men.

Suddenly an old sergeant, who sat in his saddle at the head of twenty mounted scouts, rode up to General Wessels, saluted, and said :

"General, if you let me try it I think I can get in on the flank of that rocket battery under cover of these woods and take it, if you'll keep up a fire in front till I charge, and then support me by a forward movement."

"Try it, sergeant; try it!" said the general earnestly.

In a minute the mounted scouts filed off to the rear, led by the sergeant, and were soon out of sight. The whole line now opened a heavy fire, and the men in the rocket battery had a shower of lead sent in among them at long range, to which they answered as fast as they could work their rockets. Twenty minutes passed by, and then, through his glass, General Wessels saw the scouts in the edge of the woods, not 800 yards from the rear of the battery, ready to charge, every man with his rifle at present.

The next instant, as swift as a flight of arrows, they were seen plunging forward over dry ground upon the rocketmen, and at the same instant, ceasing to fire, Wessels ordered his whole line forward with the bayonet.

The surprise was so sudden and complete that the battery and the men who worked it were in the hands of the scouts in less than a minute, and with a cheer our whole line crossed the creek and held dry ground on the other side with the captured battery in their midst. The Confederates were driven back nearly half a mile before they rallied and made it so hot for us that we had to slow up and skirmish while our guns were coming forward.

We had the rocket battery now, but none of our officers or men knew how to work it to advantage, so we could not use it on the enemy. We had to keep peppering away with rifles and muskets till near night, and then our guns were up. The Confederates then fell back to their fortified lines near Franklin, and we drew off and returned to Suffolk, pretty well worn out with Virginia mud.

And that is the brief history of the only rocket battery I ever fell in with from '61 to '65. It was rough, but not half so dangerous as it seemed, for it could not be handled like shot and shell and sent where it could do the most harm.

Farragut's Fleet Below New Orleans.—At two o'clock on the morning of April 24, 1862, a red light from the *Hartford's* taffrail warned the fleet to get under way. Positions in line of battle had been taken the night before and every ship lay "hove short" to her anchor. The fleet was formed in two divisions. That to follow up the west bank and attack Fort Jackson was the *Hartford, Brooklyn, Richmond*, and four smaller ships. That to follow the east bank and engage Fort St. Philip was the *Cayuga, Pensacola, Mississippi, Oneida, Iroquois*, and three small gunboats. The three sloops, *Hartford, Richmond* and *Brooklyn*, carried each fifteen guns in broadside, besides brass pieces in the tops.

It was a dark night, yet stars were shining. The great river boomed, for the water was high, and piles of driftwood coming down had kept all lookouts on the alert. The first division, Farragut leading, hugged the west bank as close as the *Hartford's* pilot would permit. The pilot was an old New Orleans man. He had no politics. He was working for money. He had a little cage built which let down from the port fore-chains —and dropped him just to the water's edge. His idea was to get under the smoke. Two midshipmen were stationed to signal his orders. Farragut and his staff went forward to the forecastle. Captain Wainright took the bridge, and Lieutenant Thornton, he of *Kearsarge* fame afterward, took charge of the batteries. The two lines steamed slowly up. Porter's mortars doubled their fire. The Confederate forts were silent.

There were no sounds save the swish of the current, the dull thump of the engines and the buzz and restlessness of the crew.

Farragut stood with his night-glass peering through the darkness ahead. Wainright was beside him; Watson, his signal officer, near. "Is Bailey well up in line?" he asked, without removing the glass from his eyes. "Aye, aye, sir," said the signal man softly. All at once there was a flash ahead that lit up the heavens, and in an instant a shot whistled over the *Hartford's* bow. Farragut removed the glass and said quietly, "Gentlemen, the time has come. Wainright, have your men stand by their guns. Pilot," to the man over the side, "do you see that water battery right ahead? Put this ship as close to it as you can get her." By that time the whole Confederate force was roused. Fort St. Philip opened. Fort Jackson turned loose her casements; the water battery had its whole twenty guns at play. Away ahead in the gloom could be seen the preparations of the Confederate fleet—the fire rafts being ignited, the black smoke skurrying back and forth, and withal the deadly missiles hissing by. "Port," yelled the pilot; "here we are, sir." Farragut leaned over the side. "Can't you get us any closer?" [The *Hartford* seemed then within 100 feet of the battery.] "Not without danger of grounding."

"All right. Port it is. Hard-a-port! Now, boys!" and the old man waved his glass. The crew waited for the ship to sheer, and then came the crash. It was the first broadside that had been fired in that squadron. It was deafening; it was almost paralyzing; but, like the taste of blood, the stripped sailors wanted more of it. From that hour smoke enveloped the ship. Obeying his orders, the pilot kept his ship close to the west shore. By this time the guns of Jackson were all in full play. The smoke was so dense that from the deck nothing could be seen but a sheet of flame issuing from the canopy. The fierce hail of iron from the fort was like the hiss of countless steam valves. Happily the artillerymen had poor range, and so most of their fire was ineffective. The fleet made little or no reply, but steamed ahead. Pretty soon the *Hartford*, *Richmond* and *Brooklyn* were all in position to bring their guns to bear at close range. The orders were to get as close as the pilots would allow and sweep the parapets with grape and canister. It was hardly five minutes after the ships' batteries had got into this work before the enemy's fire slackened. They could not stand it. The ships passed upward. By this time all ahead was black and fire-flamed. The Confederates had set aflame a dozen fire-rafts and they were coming down with the current.

Here was a new danger. The forts were still firing, but in the dense smoke nobody could tell where he was. A great fire-raft, the flames rising fifty feet, came swooping down on the *Hartford*. To dodge it the pilot made an error and the ship went ashore in the mud. The raft swung alongside, and in an instant the flames had caught the *Hartford's* rigging. Lieutenant Thornton's fire department was perfect, and it responded even in the face of such awful danger. The *Hartford's* engines were backed, and then it was discovered that the ram *Manassas* was pushing the fire-raft and holding it against the ship's side. "Cast loose that starboard battery!" yelled Farragut. "Quick, gentlemen! See that ram? For God's sake, give it to him!" The ram got it. The *Manassas* fell off from the raft, the raft slid by the *Hartford*, and the latter was free. Captain Warley, the commander of the *Manassas*, seeing he was hurt, tried to make for shore. The Mississippi caught him, and pushed him into the mud. There was no time to stop, or Warley would have been a prisoner, but he was helpless, and it was the duty of the wooden ships to get out of fire.

Once above the range of fire from the forts the enemy's fleet had to be encountered. It was getting almost daylight. The smoke was drifting away, and looking ahead the flag officer could see the Confederate gunboats and cotton-boats and rams. The Federal gunboat *Varuna*, Captain Boggs, had already dashed in among them, and, as the result proved, got the worst of it, for after half an hour's tussle she went down stern first and lost thirty of her crew. The *Oneida* was also being sore beset, when the heavy ships came up. Farragut, through his glass, could see at a glance where the trouble lay. The little vessels did not carry guns enough. He signaled the big ships to form in "line ahead," that is, single file, and take the middle of the channel. The Confederate fleet was formed in two lines. "Man both sides!" he called to his captain, as the

Hartford's bow loomed up through the smoke, and the *Richmond*, *Brooklyn* and *Mississippi* followed. "Man both sides!" was the signal to the other ships.

It was dreadful. As the line steamed up and the heavy batteries poured from both sides into the frail and panic-stricken craft, it seemed like horror-laden destruction. The big river steamers were all top-hamper. They had cotton bales to protect them, but the shells from the nine-inch Dahlgrens sent these flying into mid-air. Two of the craft were together. They seemed filled with people; the *Richmond* sheered within twenty feet of them and let go a broadside. The roof and cabin and "texas" and smoke-pipes all went by the board. On either bank, as the fleet passed up, were the wrecks of the wretched fleet. The officers and crews had fled. Grape and cannister from the big ships had knocked them into match kindling, and all were either sinking or burning. There was not one vessel left.

A Soldier's Bright Idea.—One day soon after Pope's defeat at second Bull Run and Chantilly, a private soldier belonging to an Ohio regiment sought an interview with his captain, and announced that he had a plan for a military campaign which must certainly result in crushing out the rebellion. The officer very naturally inquired for particulars, but the soldier refused to reveal them, and asked for a chance to lay his plans before Pope himself. After some delay he was given a pass to headquarters. He did not get to see Pope, but after the chief of staff had coaxed and promised and threatened for a quarter of an hour the Buckeye stood up and replied:

"Well, sir, my plan is for John Pope and Bob Lee to swap commands, and if we don't lick the South inside of sixty days you may shoot me for a patent hay-fork swindler!"

When he returned to camp he was naturally asked what success he met with, and ruefully replied:

"Well, they had a plan of their own."

"What was it?"

"Why, they took me out and booted me for about a mile and a half!"

Leaping from a Train.—Twenty years ago, writes Mr. J. Madison Drake, a thrilling incident occurred in the history of the writer, who at that time was a prisoner of war at Charleston, S. C. On the 6th of October, 1864, with 600 companions in misery, among them Captain Seth B. Ryder, of Elizabeth, N. J., I was *in transitu* to Columbia, the capital of the Palmetto State, being conveyed thither on a train of rickety freight cars. I had been an unwilling inmate of half a dozen prison pens for months, every attempt I had made to secure my freedom having been thwarted. Four of us studied a piece of map the night previous to setting out on this journey, and it was at a late hour that we laid ourselves down to snatch a few hours' rest. As we left the jailyard and adjoining hospital building on that bright October morning, my feelings were already "fancy free." The streets through which we silently marched on our way to the depot were as silent as the grave. Myself and three comrades—Captains Todd, Grant and Lewis—managed to take passage in the car next the "caboose," which was filled with the reserve guard, in order to evade the shots which would have been fired at us as the train passed had we jumped from a forward car. We concluded that when we reached *terra firma* the train would be some distance beyond us, and that we should be comparatively safe, and such proved to be the case. We lost no time in cultivating the acquaintance of the Confederate sergeant and his six armed guards. We distorted the truth fearfully during our brief acquaintance with these guards, in return for which they allowed my three companions to sit in the open doorway with their feet dangling outside. By sitting upon the car-floor and watching my opportunity, I was enabled to remove the percussion caps from the rifles of our unsuspecting guardians; of course this was only accomplished after vexatious delays. The removal of the last cap increased our courage and our determination to jump from the car the moment the train reached the north side of the Congaree River. We hoped for the best, and anxiously awaited the moment fraught with so much interest. The old puffing, wheezing, wood-burning locomotive was proceeding at an astonishing pace after crossing the river, and the moment for which we had been so long looking had arrived, but our hitherto buoyant hearts now almost failed us. It will not do to falter—another minute and our best opportunity will be gone—our only hope have fled. Death may await the leap which we must take, but even that was preferable to the agonizing life we were compelled to lead. The instant that Todd, a gallant Scot, upon whom we each had our eyes constantly fixed, gave the long-looked-for signal, we sprang simultaneously from the swift-moving train, and for the time, at least, were free! We had no leisure to reflect upon the terrors of our new situation. The repeated discharges of the rifles in the hands of the reserve on the last car admonished us that if we would have perfect freedom much still remained to be accomplished. But I will not here narrate how, for forty-nine long and weary days, we tramped through the swamps of South Carolina and over the snow-crested mountains of North Carolina, and finally, after passing through a thousand dangers, reached in safety the beautiful and historic city of Knoxville, having accomplished a march of over one thousand miles.

A Funny Story at a Solemn Time.—Just before the battle of Fredericksburg, writes a gentleman who was intimately connected with Mr. Lincoln's administration, knowing that a large number of Pennsylvania troops were with Burnside, and that a general engagement between the two armies was imminent, I went to Washington and asked for transportation to the front. A tug was placed at my disposal, and I reached the army in time to witness the battle. The terrible slaughter of our troops on that disastrous day we all know.

When our defeat was beyond question, I boarded the tug and hastened to Washington, hoping, as railroad communication was impossible, to forestall the exaggerated rumors that might be expected, and to alleviate even in only a slight degree the shock of unwelcome tidings. It was considerably past midnight when I reached Washington, but I proceeded directly to the White House. It was no surprise to me to learn that the

President had not retired. I was immediately ushered into his presence. As he accosted me and read in my face the character of the news I had to communicate, he sank into a chair with a sigh of distress.

"What news, Governor?" said he.

"Bad! very bad."

"Tell me all!" He rested his head on his hands while I gave the outline and the results of the battle. He heaved a heavy sigh and looked at me with an expression of intense suffering, and I remarked:

"I heartily wish I might be a welcome messenger of good news instead—that I could tell you how to conquer or get rid of these rebellious States."

Looking up quickly, with a marked change of expression, Lincoln said:

"That reminds me of two boys in Illinois, who took a short cut across an orchard, and did not become aware of the presence of a vicious dog until it was too late to reach either fence. One was spry enough to escape the attack by climbing a tree, but the other started around a tree, with the dog in hot pursuit, until, by making smaller circles than it was possible for his pursuer to make, he gained sufficiently to grasp the dog's tail, and held with desperate grip until nearly exhausted, when he hailed his companion and called to him to come down.

"'What for?' said the boy.

"'I want you to help me let this dog go.'

"If I could only let them go," said the President in conclusion; "but that is the trouble. I am compelled to hold on to them and make them stay."

Stories About Shiloh.—"The strangest experiences at Shiloh," said one of the listeners at a recent sitting of veterans of the war, "were among the wounded after the battle. There was one case that came under my own observation. Major Oliver Denslow was surgeon of a Missouri regiment, and was caring for the wounded on one of the boats. He came to a volunteer of a Wisconsin regiment who had made a quick trip from his home and who had joined his regiment just in time for the battle. This man had been wounded in the foot, and the surgeon was amputating the shattered member, when he discovered that the wounded soldier was Oliver Denslow Pease, his nephew, whom he had not seen for eighteen years."

"Speaking of Nelson," said another one of the quintet, "I saw him meet his match on one occasion. He was given to superintending personally the crossing of rivers, and on one occasion he made eight men jump into the water and drag out a half-drowned mule. After an experience of this kind he came upon a wagon train stuck in the mud. Major Igo, Quartermaster of the Thirty-fifth Indiana regiment, was working as hard as a man could work to get the wagons out, and had his men in position for a lift when Nelson rode up. Pushing his way up close to the major, Nelson roared out: 'Blank you, sir, what's the matter with that wagon?" Raising his hot face, the major roared back: 'You get out of this, blank you. The wagon's stuck in the mud. Any blank fool can see that.' 'Do you know who I am, sir? Do you know who I am, sir?' shouted Nelson in a fury. 'Certainly I do,' responded the major. 'You are the Quartermaster of that Ohio Regiment in front, and you can't boss me around. Nobody but old Nelson himself can do that.' After receiving this reply Nelson indulged in a chuckle and rode away."

President Lincoln and Mr. Duff Green.—The following interesting incident of Mr. Lincoln's visit to Richmond is related by Admiral Porter in the *Century Magazine*: As we lay below Richmond in the flagship *Malvern*, a man appeared at the landing dressed in gray homespun, with a somewhat decayed appearance, and with a staff about six feet long in his hand. It was, in fact, nothing more than a stick taken from a wood-pile. It was two and a half inches in diameter, and was not even smoothed at the knots. It was just such a weapon as a man would pick up to kill a mad dog with.

"Who are you, and what do you want?" asked the officer of the deck. "You cannot come on board unless you have important business."

"I am Duff Green," said the man. "I want to see Abraham Lincoln, and my business concerns myself alone. You tell Abraham Lincoln Duff Green wants to see him."

The officer came down into the cabin and delivered the message. I arose and said: "I will go up and send him away." But the President said: "Let him come on board. Duff is an old friend of mine, and I would like to talk to him."

I then went on deck to have a boat sent for him, and to see what kind of a man this was who sent off such arrogant messages to the President of the United States. He stepped into the boat as if it belonged to him; instead of sitting down, he stood up, leaning on his long staff. When he came over the side he stood on the deck defiantly, looked up at the flag and scowled, and then turning to me (whom he knew very well), he said, "I want to see Abraham Lincoln." He paid no courtesy to me or to the quarter deck.

It had been a very long time since he had shaved or cut his hair, and he might have come under the head of "unkempt and not canny."

"When you come," I said, "in a respectful manner, the President will see you; but throw away that cord of wood you have in your hand before entering the President's presence."

"How long is it," he said, "since Abraham Lincoln took to aping royalty? Man, dressed in brief authority, cuts such fantastic capers before high Heaven that it makes angels weep. I can expect airs from a naval officer, but I don't expect to find them in a man of Abraham Lincoln's horse sense."

I thought the man crazy, and think so still. "I can't permit you to see the President," I said, "until I receive further instructions; but you can't see him at all until you throw that wood-pile overboard."

He turned on his heel and tried to throw the stick on shore, but it fell short and went floating down the current.

"Ah!" he said, "has it come to that? Is he afraid of assassination? Tyrants generally get into that condition!"

I went down and reported this queer customer to the President, and told him I thought the man crazy, but he said, "Let him come down; he always was a little queer. I sha'n't mind him." Mr. Duff Green was shown into the cabin. The President got up from his chair to receive him, and, approaching him, offered him his hand. "No," said Green, with a tragic air, "it is red with blood; I can't touch it. When I knew it, it was an honest hand. It has cut the throats of thousands of my people, and their blood, which now lies soaking into the ground, cries aloud to Heaven for vengeance. I came to see you, not for old remembrance' sake, but to give you a piece of my opinion. You won't like it, but I don't care, for people don't generally like to have the truth told them. You have come here, protected by your army and navy, to gloat over the ruin and desolation you have caused. You are a second Nero, and had you lived in his day you would have fiddled while Rome was burning!"

When the fanatic commenced this tirade of abuse Mr. Lincoln was standing with his hand outstretched, his mouth wreathed with the pleasant smile he almost always wore, and his eyes lighted up as when anything pleased him. He was pleased because he was about to meet an old and esteemed friend, and better pleased that he had come to see him of his own accord.

Mr. Lincoln gradually withdrew his outstretched hand as Duff Green started on his talk; the smile left his lips as the talker got to the middle of his harangue, and the softness of his eyes faded out. He was another man altogether.

Had any one shut his eyes after Duff Green commenced speaking and opened them when he stopped, he would have seen a perfect transformation. His slouchy position had disappeared, his mouth was compressed, his eyes were fixed, and he looked four inches taller than usual.

Duff Green went on without noticing the change in the President's manner and appearance. "You came here," he continued, "to triumph over a poor conquered town, with only women and children in it; whose soldiers have left it and would rather starve than see your hateful presence here;—those soldiers—and only a handful at that—who have four years defied your paid mercenaries on these glorious hills and have taught you to respect the rights of the South. You have given your best blood to conquer them, and now you will march back to your demoralized capital and lay out your wits to win them over so that you can hold this Government in perpetuity. Shame on you! Shame on—"

Mr. Lincoln could stand it no longer. His coarse hair stood on end and his nostrils dilated like those of an excited race-horse. He stretched out his long right arm and extended his lean forefinger until it almost touched Duff Green's face. He made one step forward to place himself as near as possible to his vituperator, and in a clear, cutting voice addressed him. He was really graceful while he was speaking—the grace of one who is expressing his honest convictions. "Stop, you political tramp," he exclaimed; "you, the aider and abettor of those who have brought all this ruin on your country, without the courage to risk your person in defense of the principles you profess to espouse. A fellow who stood by to gather up the loaves and fishes if any should fall to you. A man who had no principles in the North, and who took none South with him. A political hyena, who robbed the graves of the dead and adopted their language as his own. You talk of the North cutting the throats of the Southern people! You have all cut your own throats, and, unfortunately, cut many of those of the North. Miserable impostor, vile intruder, go, before I forget myself and the high position I hold! Go, I tell you, and don't desecrate this National vessel another minute!" And he made a step toward him.

This was something which Duff Green had not calculated upon. He had never seen Abraham Lincoln in anger. His courage failed him, and he turned and fled out of the cabin and up the cabin stairs as if the avenging angel was after him. He never stopped until he reached the gangway, and there he stood looking at the shore, seemingly measuring the distance to see if he could swim to the landing.

I was close behind him, and when I got on deck, I said to the officer in charge:

"Put that man on shore, and if he appears in sight of this vessel while we are here, have him sent away with scant ceremony."

He was as humble at that moment as a whipped dog, and hurried into the boat. The last I saw of him he was striding rapidly over the fields as if to reach the shelter of the woods. The man must have been deranged. When I returned to the cabin, about fifteen minutes later, the President was perfectly calm, as if nothing had happened.

A Daring Confederate Officer.—Lord Burgoyne, of England, relates the following story: "In the summer of 1863, I was cruising in my yacht, the *Greyhound*, in the waters of the English Channel and the Mediterranean. One day I ran into Cherbourg, France. The town was alive with excitement. The Confederate cruiser *Alabama* had been followed into the harbor by the United States man-of-war *Kearsarge*. The two hostile vessels were lying scarcely a cable's length apart. Under the neutrality law, twenty-four hours must elapse after the departure of one before the other would be allowed to follow. Captain Winslow, of the *Kearsarge*, had sent a challenge to Captain Semmes, of the *Alabama*, for a naval duel outside of the harbor. Captain Semmes was anxious to avoid a fight, but, as you remember, was eventually forced into it.

"That evening at the table d'hôte I sat beside a gentleman who proved to be an American. He was obviously a man of the world, refined and cultivated. After chatting pleasantly, I remarked that I had been invited to visit the *Kearsarge* the next day. My new-found friend expressed a desire to accompany me. I consented, and together we went on board. The officers were very courteous, and apparently took great pleasure in showing us about the ship. My friend manifested the liveliest interest in everything he saw. His minute inquiries into the number of men carried, weight of armament, etc., showed an intelligent understanding of nautical matters that delighted our entertainers and elicited from them the information desired.

"A few days later both vessels steamed out of the harbor, and the celebrated fight took place. My sympathies were naturally with the South, and I sailed as close to the scene of action as was compatible with safety, to render what services I could to the crew of the Confederate cruiser. After the sinking of the *Alabama*, I succeeded in rescuing a score of the survivors. Among the number were Semmes and his first officer. As the latter stood before me, wet and shivering from his cold bath, my eyes opened with astonishment. 'Why,' said I, 'this is Mr. ———. naming my friend of the table d'hôte and fellow-visitor to the *Kearsarge*.' 'Yes,' was the laughing reply, 'and I had her boilers located so that we would have put a shot through them in another minute if she hadn't sunk us when she did.'"

Reminiscences of Gettysburg.—My last visit to this place, writes a newspaper correspondent, was in July, 1863, when I was compelled by force of circumstances to witness the grandest battle ever fought on this continent. I am now seated on the spot where I then stood and viewed the famous charge that resulted so disastrously to Lee's forces. I see around me the identical rocks behind which the tired-out troops of part of the old Fifth Corps patiently awaited the orders to "wade in." On my left is the place where Haslett's Battery was in position, and I can imagine I hear the thunder of its guns and see the devastation it created in the onward moving lines of Pickett's troops. I see the very stone upon which General Weed was leaning when he received his death-wound, and in my mind's eye I see the gallant Haslett take him in his arms, and the next moment receive the bullet that left the famous battery without a captain. Across Plumb Run is the rugged pile of rocks called "Devil's Den," and a devil's den it was. 'Twas there the rebel sharpshooters were safely posted, and with Enfield rifles shot down our officers as fast as they made themselves visible. I imagine I see the handful of soldiers of the One Hundred and Fifty-fifth Pennsylvania Volunteers—all from the old city of smoke—dashing across the muddy creek and pushing on pell-mell until the devils in the den were either killed or captured. I have in my possession a photograph taken of this spot immediately after the battle, and the piles of Union and Rebel dead intermingled tell a story that language fails to describe. What horrid sights they were! Over beyond is where Sweitzer's brigade changed front to the right, and had a hand-to-hand struggle with a force superior in numbers, and as the gallant men moved diagonally across the field, pouring volley after volley into the enemy, the reserves charged down upon the flank of the gray-backed horde and drove them from the field. But a short distance to my right is where Judge Collier (then Colonel) formed his regiment—the One Hundred and Thirty-ninth Pennsylvania Volunteers. He was wounded there shortly after, and it is not far to the spot where old Captain Sample received the wound that caused his death. He was a very old man when he entered the service, but the blood of his father, who did yeoman duty in the war of 1812, ran through his veins, and, as Judge Collier said, "A braver old man never died for his country." How vividly all these events appear, and yet they happened more than twenty years ago.

A Pine Woods Ball in Northern Alabama During the War.—The following incident is related by Edwin Ledyard, an ex-Confederate scout, in the Philadelphia *Times*: "There were lighter shades to the picture of life on Sand Mountain and its vicinity. Here is one of them. Imagine a lonely and solitary horseman (after the manner of G. P. R. James' heroes) riding along the road between Asheville, St. Clair County, and Gadsden. The shades of evening had closed decidedly, and naught was heard but the voice of the katydid and the occasional screech of the owl. The solitary rider, who was your humble servant, was tired and hungry. He had been in the saddle since early morning and had not had a meal the whole day. It was with feelings of pleasure, then, that he saw a light by the roadside. As he approached it he saw that it proceeded from the open door of a log-cabin, from which came the melodious sounds of a fiddle. The sound of the horse's tramp brought several of the natives to the door. 'Stranger, won't you 'light?' exclaimed one of them.

"The stranger 'lit,' and, fastening his horse, entered the cabin. Here a scene of revelry by night presented itself. The room was lighted by pine knots burning in the fire-place. The floor was made of puncheons, and was by no means as smooth as the surface of the conventional ball-room. None the less, about two dozen young men and maidens were tripping it merrily. The music was furnished by the young men in turn, most of whom seemed to have some knowledge of the fiddle. The young ladies from time to time would go to the fire to warm their feet, which caused me to make the astounding discovery that none of them wore stockings.

"The dance was a mixture of a Virginia reel, an Irish jig and a sailor's hornpipe. I have never seen the like since. I was introduced to the belle of the ball as a distinguished stranger, and I was sufficiently fortunate to engage her as a partner for the next dance. Well, we danced, and at the conclusion of our going up and down the middle my fair partner faced me with her arms akimbo. I saw we were to perform a *pas de deux*, and that she proposed to dance me down. My soul rose in arms; the honor of the Confederate army was at stake, and at it we went.

"I am generally regarded as a truthful man, and I wouldn't like to say positively how high that girl jumped from the floor. I think it was three feet when she tried. She danced me down, there's no denying it, and then started off with another partner as fresh as a daisy. I didn't wait till the close of the ball. The refreshments were not to my taste, consisting principally of cold bacon and greens, spring water and pine-top whisky, and I was soon on my way again."

President Grant and the Old Sailor.—The following is not an anecdote of the Rebellion, but it is told of one who, with the exception of Mr. Lincoln, is more fondly remembered in connection with the great struggle than any other, and, as it is too good to be lost, we will make a place for it. It is related by ex-Secretary of the Navy Robeson :

"When I was Secretary of the Navy, some hundreds of the sailors of the better class came to me and asked to have some rank given them. They didn't care about an increase of pay, they said, but they wanted relative rank.

"I couldn't do anything for them, but they came several times, and were rather importunate, and I finally led a delegation of them over to the White House and let them present their petition to President Grant in person. They told him what they wanted, and argued for a redress of their grievances plainly but forcibly.

"At last, an old boatswain came to the front, and, hitching up his trousers and turning over his incumbent quid, he said: 'Mr. President, I can put this 'ere matter so's you can see it plain. Now, here I be—a parent; in fact, a father. My son is a midshipman. He outranks me, don't you observe? That ain't right, don't you see?'

"'Indeed,' said Grant; 'who appointed him a middy?'

"'The Secretary here,' the bo'sun said; and encouraged by the question, he went on: 'It ain't right, don't you see, that I should be beneath 'im? W'y, ef I was to go on to his ship, the boy I brought up to ob-jence would boss his own father! Just think of that!'

"'An' he has better quarters'n me, and better grub, nice furn'ture, an' all that; sleeps in a nice soft bed'n all that. See?'

"'Yes,' said the President; 'yes, the world is full of inequalities. I know of a case quite similar to yours.'

"The old bo'sun chuckled quietly, and gave another hitch to his lower gear.

"'I know of an old fellow,' said General Grant, 'who is postmaster of a little town in Kentucky. He lives in a plain way, in a small house. He is a nice old man, but he isn't much in rank. His son outranks him more than your son does. His son lives in Washington in the biggest house there, and he is surrounded by the nicest of furniture, and eats and drinks anything he takes a notion to. He could remove his father from office in a minute if he wanted to. But he doesn't want to. And the old man—that's Jesse Grant, you know—doesn't seem to care about the inequality in rank. I suppose he is glad to see his boy get along in the world.'

"The old bo'sun looked down at the carpet, and tried to bore a hole in it with his toe, and his comrades all laughed at him joyously, and slapped him on the back, and filed out in great glee. It was the last I ever heard of the petition or the petitioners. The old bo'sun flung his quid into a cuspidor as he left. Probably he had concluded to give up thinking."

One of the Miracles of War.—No complete history of the war of the Rebellion will ever be written. To write such a history one would have to record the deeds of more than two million veterans who participated in that memorable struggle for the life of the greatest nation that ever existed on the globe. As an instance of the hundreds of thousands of thrilling incidents that were of every-day occurrence in the lives of the brave men who for four years bravely battled for their country, we would record the following narrow escape of D. W. Butler, who was a member of Company A, Ninety-second Illinois mounted infantry. On the morning of the 23d of April, 1864, the company was on picket duty in front of Sherman's grand army, which, within a few days, was to commence its victorious advance upon Atlanta and the grand march to the sea. The advance position held by our pickets was twenty miles south of Chattanooga, and Johnson's army was in their immediate front to dispute further advance. Under cover of darkness, a force of rebels took position in front of the Union vedettes, while another force penetrated to their rear and erected a barricade across the road. When the rebel fire was opened the vedettes were ordered to fall back, and in doing this fell into the rebel ambush. Seeing the trap into which they had fallen, Butler determined that his only chance of escape was to leap the barricade, and urging his horse to the top of his speed, he guided him, in the face of the rebel fire, for that position, which was soon reached, and horse and rider cleared the barricade, only to fall on the other side, the former fatally shot and the latter stunned and senseless from the fall. To make sure of their victim, the rebels then with the butts of their muskets crushed his skull. This occurred at four o'clock in the morning, and at ten o'clock the position was retaken by our troops, and the Federal dead, among them Butler, were thrown into a wagon and removed to the rear. In a casual examination of the bodies, the surgeon discovered signs of life in Butler, and he was taken to the hospital, where he received proper attention, and on the 9th of May, sixteen days after this occurrence, he returned to consciousness.

"Forty Rounds, U. S."—On the return of the Fifteenth Corps from the relief of Knoxville, after having marched all the way from Memphis and back to Chattanooga, a soldier of the Eighth Missouri—one of Sherman's bummers, an Irishman who had been a roustabout on the levees of St. Louis—came straggling along behind the column on a cold, dreary day for that section; his knapsack slung on one shoulder, his blanket over the other; across his breast and tied at his left hip, a greasy but empty haversack; his pants worn and rent in many places, and in others sewed up with cord; no peak to his cap, his musket at "reversed arms," and altogether presenting the appearance of general disgust and demoralization. Off from the road he was attracted by a headquarters tent and sentinel in a neat and comfortable uniform, whom he approached and accosted, when the following dialogue ensued:

"I say, sintinil, could ye tell me where me rigiment is?"

"What regiment do you belong to?"

"Eighth Misshory, sure."

"What division?"

"Morgan Ill [L.] Smit's, av coorse."

"What brigade?"

"Phwat brigade? Faith, an' don't ye know it's Giles Smit's—the Sucund Brigade of Morgan Ill's Division?"

"What corps is it in?"

"Phwat coor is it?. Ah, thin, ye blackguard, do'sint everybody know that it's in the Fifteenth Coor?"

"How could I tell what corps you belonged to when you have no corps badge?"

"Noa badge, is it?—Coor badge! Now, thin, phwat's a coor badge?"

"Do you see that crescent on my partner's hat? Well, that's

the badge of his corps—the Eleventh ; and this star on my cap is the badge of my corps—the Twelfth."

"Ho, ho! I see, now. Thim's the lights yez Potomac byes have to show home some dark nights. Yez takes the moon and sthars along wid yez "

Laughing at the witty remark, the sentinel responded: " Well, what's the badge of your corps?"

Hesitating a moment to gather a thought, then making a left face and slapping his right hand on his cartridge box, the Irishman replied, "D'ye see that?" [Then a moment's pause.] "Forty rounds in my cartridge box and twenty in my pocket —that's the badge of Logan's Fifteenth Coor, do yez mind that! that kem all the way from Vicksburg to help yez Potomac fellows foight at Chattanoogy."

The incident having been related to General Logan the same evening by an officer who overheard it, the cartridge box, bearing the legend "40 Rounds, U. S.," was at once adopted by General Logan as the corps badge, and a general order to that effect issued next day.

A Remarkable Soldier.—One of the most remarkable private soldiers on either side of the late war was a young man named Tom Kelly, of the Second Michigan Infantry. The remarkable began with his build. He had arms a full hand longer than any man who could be found. He had no more backbone than a snake, and could almost tie himself in a knot. He could tell the date on a silver quarter held up twenty feet away.

When Tom's remarkable qualifications were discovered, he was detailed as a scout and spy, and was changed from one department to another. In the capacity of a spy he entered Richmond three times. He entered Vicksburg and preached a sermon to the soldiers a week before that city was taken. He was a man who firmly believed that he could not be killed by an enemy, and he governed his movements accordingly. During his three and a half years in the service, Kelly captured fifty-two Confederates and turned them over as prisoners. He was captured and escaped five times. . As a spy, he entered more than thirty Confederate camps and forts. He was fired upon at least one thousand times, and yet was never wounded. He said that he would never die by the hand of an enemy, and his prophecy came true. In the last year of the war, while bringing a captured Confederate scout into camp, both were killed within forty rods of the Union lines by a bolt of lightning.

Lincoln's Visit to Richmond.—Admiral Porter's reminiscences of Abraham Lincoln's visit to Richmond, says the Springfield (Mass.) *Republican*, find eager readers in the old soldiers of the country, and one of them—Capt. Z. C. Warren, of this city—adds a picturesque incident to the story. As drawn by Admiral Porter, the scenes of Lincoln's passage from the wharf at Richmond, where the gunboat *Malvern* left them together, to General Weitzel's headquarters, in the house vacated two days before by Jeff Davis, are picturesque in their portrayal of the feelings of the negroes. It was hardly to be expected that the whites, even if Union men, with their more reserved temperaments, would give way to any such transports of emotion. But Captain Warren relates an instance which epitomizes the joy and relief felt by the Union men who had lived at the South during the war. Captain Warren, whose gunners had been the first artillerymen to enter the evacuated city, as officer of the day, was early among the visitors at a reception which Mr. Lincoln held for a couple of hours in the parlor of the old Davis house for the soldiers and loyal Richmond people. The President was bearing the journey well, though his inevitable black frock coat and "stovepipe" hat were a bit the worse for travel. A few officers had been introduced, and some of them stood chatting about the room, Captain Warren among them, when General Weitzel came out of a rear room with a tall, lank civilian, gray-haired, and plainly a man of prominence. Leading him up to Mr. Lincoln, the General introduced him as a great friend of John Minor Botts, and a Union man whose loyalty the past few years had cost him persecution. As the President turned to greet the stranger, a great throb of emotion shook the old man's frame, and quickly stepping forward he flung his arms about

Mr. Lincoln's neck in the most tragic manner. "Thank God I have lived to see this day!" he cried. The small audience in uniform, touched at the sight, watched it with interested eyes. The old civilian seemed to forget the place, the President, his attitude and everything, and the situation was fast becoming ridiculous. Mr. Lincoln, ever quick to see the humorous side of anything, interposed. With a kindly smile passing over his angular features, he gently released himself from the grasp of Mr. Botts' friend, remarking, "About how tall are you, sir?" The sound of his voice awoke the old man from his reflections and quickly turned the current of his thoughts. Recollecting himself at once, the tall stranger replied, stating his height, which Lincoln declared to be two inches less than his own. The old man stepped aside, evidently quite unconscious of the mingled pathos and humor of the little scene in which he had played so prominent a part. Capt. Warren remained in Richmond about ten days longer, and, returning after a short march South, was mustered out there in June, still wearing on his sword the knot of crape which the officers were ordered to place there for 60 days in memory of the martyr President. He has never taken it off.

Gen. Sickles' Lost Leg.—Ex-Police Commissioner General Duryea was philosophizing a few days ago over a glass of wine. His thoughts were on the compensations of life, and were suggested by the presence of a most genial little gentleman who had the misfortune to have no legs. "I have no doubt," said one who was present, "that the loss of a limb, or the loss of sight or hearing, has some sort of compensation in the effect on the loser's habits, mode of life, his nature, moods or disposition. At any rate, I never see a lame, blind or deaf person that I do not wonder what sort of person he or she was before the loss." "The case of General Sickles is a double illustration," said the General. "I happen to know that General Meade strongly condemned him for disobedience of orders in making the movement which brought on the battle of Gettysburg. He expressed his condemnation in my hearing, and Sickles would have been court-martialed if he had not lost his leg in that fight. But he not only escaped court-martial, but found renewed favor in military eyes by that loss. Moreover, the lo s changed Sickles' whole methods of life and his nature in some degree, making a more serious, earnest man of him." I recalled and mentioned that over a camp-fire in Georgia, in 1864, General Sickles told me that he made the movement which precipitated that battle purposely, and under the belief that General Meade intended to retreat from his position. "I brought on a battle," he said, "not a retreat, and it was a victory; but," he added, looking down at his stump of a leg, " I paid very dearly for it."

A Story of General McCook.—The following is from "Curb-Stone Crayons," in the Chicago Inter-Ocean:

"One story brings on another," said Colonel E. S. Watts the other day. Some one had told a story of McCook at Perryville, and the Colonel, who had at one time commanded the Second Kentucky Cavalry, starting with the remark quoted above, continued in this wise: "I remember McCook very well. There was one thing he did that I have never been able to charge up to him quite to my own satisfaction.

"One of our men, named Richardson, had for some misdemeanor been sentenced to carry a fence-rail for a given number of hours in front of regimental headquarters. Richardson made the best of it, and he had not been very long on duty when McCook and staff rode by. As they passed, Richardson came to a front face, brought his rail down to a present arms, and stood like a statue. Some of the officers laughed, but General McCook wheeled his horse and rode straight down on the man.

"Reining in his horse a few feet from the rail-bearer, he asked: 'What's your name?' Promptly came the answer: 'Private R chardson, of the Second Kentucky Cavalry.' The General directed him to call the sergeant of the guard. When the sergeant came, McCook asked for how long the man was to carry the rail. As the sergeant answered twenty-four hours, Richardson was in great glee. He imagined the General was about to order his release, but instead, McCook said: 'Make it forty-eight, blank him!' and rode away."

"That was like McCook," said Captain Blume, of the Second Kentucky Infantry. "I'll bet Richardson rather liked the General for rebuking his smartness."

A Confederate Soldier's Pride.—On the occasion of the Federal advance to Stone River, or Murfreesboro, the Confederates drew back to a line of battle. On the retreat a young Confederate soldier fell, and a heavy rail struck him across the thighs, but he managed to crawl up to two stacks of straw and drag himself between them for concealment. While here he was found by Jack Norris, a stalwart six-footer of the Fifth Kentucky (Federal) infantry, who had been detailed as a stretcher-bearer. Norris repeatedly ordered the young rebel to surrender, and was as often answered by the snapping of a gun which would not go off. Colonel Treanor, hearing the cursing of Norris, hurried to the scene, and the young soldier at once said he would surrender to a soldier, but not to an infernal stretcher-bearer. The prisoner was a handsome boy of sixteen, and a nephew of the Confederate General Wood. The large-hearted Yankee colonel took the boy under his protection, conceived a great liking for him, shared his sweet-potato supper with him, spooned under the same blanket, and bade him "good-bye" at last with real regret.

This incident illustrates soldierly pride, and brings to recollection the many amenities between soldiers on different sides, which had a tendency to soften asperities of war into questions of patriotic duty.

A Reporter's Adventures at Gettysburg.—Mr. A. H. Byington, editor of the Norwalk (Conn.) *Gazette*, was during three years of the war a Washington and field correspondent of the New York *Tribune*. He relates the following story: "It was the latter part of June, 1863, that I got a dispatch from Culpeper Court House to hurry out there, for our army was on the move. I went at once, but the army had already started north at a rapid pace, trying to keep between the rebel army and Washington. Hooker was in command. I went to the headquarters of Meade, who was stationed at Goose Creek. He told me there was going to be a battle, but my best way was to go back to Washington and hurry up to Harper's Ferry, and there I would head off the army and find the Seventeenth Connecticut, whose quartermaster had one of my horses.

"When I got to Harper's Ferry I found Hooker in a fume. I soon learned that he had demanded to have the 10,000 inactive men on Bolivar Heights attached to his own army for the battle with Lee, and that Halleck had refused. Hooker resigned that afternoon, and Lincoln commissioned Meade to command the Army of the Potomac. The Seventeenth Connecticut was still ahead of me. General Bob Tyler, of the Connecticut brigade, was there, and he took my map and marked a red ring around on it on the Pennsylvania line, and said, 'within a few days there would be within that circle one of the biggest fights the world ever saw. Go around to Baltimore and head it off at York, Pa.'

"Again I followed directions. I tried Baltimore, but news came there that the rebels had burned the bridges and torn up the track. I finally went to Philadelphia and got to York by way of Lancaster, determined to be the first reporter on the ground. The track was torn up, but I got a minister to carry me twelve miles in his wagon. J. E. B. Stuart's rebel cavalry had been to York, gutted the provision stores and taken $20,000 from the bank. Occasionally I heard a gun go off in the southwest. I hired a buggy, telling the owner to charge it to the *Tribune* if I never came back, and drove in the direction of the cannonading.

"I drove away twelve miles, encountering some rebel cavalry on the way, and got to Hanover. There had been a severe cavalry fight there. The town had a disorderly appearance; people stayed close in their houses, and the *débris* of arms and accoutrements lay along the roads. The wounded were gathered in the church. Telegraph wires were broken and strewn around.

"I stopped at the hotel and asked the landlord if there was no telegraph operator there. 'Yes, there he is,' said he, pointing out a little hunchback named Tone. I asked him where his battery was. 'At home under the bed,' he said. 'The wires are all cut and there is no use trying to telegraph.' After considerable parleying I got some men to go out on a handcar and fix the wires, I paying the men and making myself responsible for the value of the car. Then the battery was brought out and we got Baltimore, the operator promising an absolute monopoly of the wire for two days.

"Then I hurried to the battle-field, some five miles off. Before reaching there I met General Howard and he told me of the first day's fight, of Reynolds' death and many other things. I found J. R. Sypher, whom I had engaged at Lancaster to follow me, and we sent off by our private telegraph wire an account of the fight of the first two days. It was a magnificent feat. No other accounts got through that night, and between 9:30 and midnight the *Tribune* sold 65,000 copies on the streets of the city.

"Tone kept getting the strange signal 'K. I.' 'K. I.' 'What the dickens does 'K. I.' mean?' he asked. 'I'm afraid the rebs have tapped our wire.' Finally he found out that it was the War Department at Washington. 'We have got Byington's first despatch,' said Stanton, 'and it is our first news. Send along more. We are listening.' For two days I sent exclusive dispatches over my wire, giving all particulars of the great battle, while the *Herald* was running relays of horses. I telegraphed that the railroad was whole from Baltimore to Hanover, and the government sent out trains for our wounded. The surgeon told me that that railroad saved Gen. Sickles' life.

"After the battle I got a horse and hurried on after the rebels, wondering that Meade did not pursue. They were all broken up and demoralized, the roadside strewn with sick men, with dead horses and abandoned weapons. Next day I came up with Lee's main army. It was huddled together in 'a horseshoe-shaped bend of the Potomac—in a valley surrounded by hills on one side and by the swollen and rushing river on the other. It would have been easy to bag them all. Their flight was fatally interrupted. The pontoons they had crossed on were swept away, and they had no means to recross. By a friend who had accompanied me I sent back to President Lincoln and the *Tribune* the somewhat premature dispatch: 'We've got Lee's army tight. It cannot escape.'

"After waiting there a while I turned back to meet Meade's army, which I supposed must be rapidly approaching up the road. In vain I looked and waited. It did not appear. Well, you know the rest.

"I was at Washington when Meade came to report after the battle of Gettysburg. I asked Gideon Wells, Secretary of the Navy, about the interview. 'I was present in the Cabinet,' he said, ' when General Meade came to tell about the battle, and take counsel about the situation. "Do you know, General," Mr. Lincoln suddenly broke out, with a laugh, " what your attitude toward Lee for a week after the battle of Gettysburg reminded me of." "No, Mr. President, what is it?" asked Meade. "I could think of nothing else," said Lincoln, " than an old woman trying to shoo her geese across the creek!"' After that Meade never quite recovered confidence."

Mr. Lincoln's Joke Upon Secretary Chase.—Just after the publication of Secretary Chase's exceedingly able Treasury report in 1863, and when the Secretary was known to have the Presidential bee buzzing in his bonnet, a zealous friend of the President went to him (Lincoln) with a suggestion that Mr. Chase should be looked after ; he was using his power as Secretary of the Treasury to further his own ambitious schemes. Lincoln laughed shrewdly and brought out the inevitable story of which he was reminded. An Illinois farmer, tilling a few acres of land and employing only one poor old horse, was plowing one day, while his son regarded the operation from the nearest fence. Suddenly the old, spiritless horse pricked up his ears and started briskly onward in the furrow, almost dragging the old man at the plow-tail around the land. The lad surveyed the unusual sight from the fence, the old man having hard work to keep up as the horse went flying around, and then he cried out : " Say, dad, why don't you brush off that gad-fly on old Dobbin's back ?" As he flew past the old man replied : " I never saw Dobbin doing so well before. Let the gad-fly be." How Lincoln made the application any man can tell.

General Sheridan's Story of Read's Famous Poem.—Referring to the poem of "Sheridan's Ride," the General was asked if he had ever met the author.

"Yes," he replied, "I know him well. I first met him at the battle of Stone River. He was a guest at the headquarters of General Rosecrans, and stayed with us a good while."

"Did you know how he happened to write it?"

"Yes, I have heard him tell about it a great many times. There are a number of stories floating around, but I'll give you the true one, as Read told it to me. James E. Murdoch suggested the idea."

"Murdoch, the elocutionist?"

"Yes; he was an actor at one of the Cincinnati theatres at the time, and a great friend of mine. He lost a son at the battle of Missionary Ridge—Murdoch did—and came down there to get the body. The enemy occupied the place where the boy was buried, and the old man remained there a guest at my headquarters. He used to ride the lines with me, and always used the black horse Rienzi, that was afterward called Winchester, and became very fond of him. Things were very exciting down there, and Murdoch saw a good deal of war. Sundays he always read and recited poems to the troops around headquarters, and there was one poem of Browning's that was always called for. It was a great favorite with the soldiers, and with me, and we never let him off without reading it. It was the ride from Ghent to Aix—you remember it?"

"Well, after the battle of Cedar Creek, there was published in *Harper's Weekly* a story of my ride from Winchester, and a picture of me on the black horse Rienzi. Murdoch saw it and took it up to Read, suggesting that it was a good theme for a poem. Murdoch had just seen an officer who was there and gave him a description of the affair, and Read jumped at the idea. He shut himself up in his room, wrote the poem that afternoon, had his wife make a copy, and sent it over to Murdoch's house as soon as it was done, to see how he liked it. Murdoch was very much pleased, and that night read the poem at the theatre between the acts."

"So it got into the newspapers, where I first saw it."

"It is said you have the original manuscript?"

"No; I never saw it."

"How did Read happen to paint the picture?"

"He did it on an order from the Union League Club of Philadelphia. They sent him down to New Orleans, where I was stationed, and I sat for him there. He was going to Rome that fall and could not finish it, but made some sketches and completed the picture at Rome. I never had a copy of the picture, but he afterward gave me the sketches, which I still have at my house."

"Who were with you on that ride?"

"Sandy Forsythe and Colonel O'Keefe, of my staff. Forsythe is down in New Mexico now, lieutenant-colonel of the Fourth Cavalry. O'Keefe was killed at the battle of Five Forks."

A Daring Naval Exploit.—The following graphic description of the famous engagement at Island No. 10 is extracted from an article by Rear Admiral Walke in the *Century Magazine*:

"Having received written orders from the flag officer, under date of March 30, I at once began to prepare the *Carondelet* for the ordeal. All the loose material at hand was collected, and on April 4 the vessels' decks were covered with it, to protect them against plunging shot. Hawsers and chain cables were placed around the pilot house and other vulnerable parts of the vessel, and every precaution was adopted to prevent disaster. A coal barge, laden with hay and coal, was lashed to the part of the port side on which there was no iron plating, to protect the magazine. And it was truly said that the old *Carondelet* at that time resembled a farmer's wagon prepared for market. The engineers led the escape-steam through the pipes aft, into the wheel-house, to avoid the puffing sound it made when blown through the smoke-stacks.

"All the necessary preparations having been made, I informed the flag officer of my intention to run the gantlet that night and received his approval. Colonel Buford, who commanded the land forces temporarily with the flotilla, assisted me in preparing for the trip, and on the night of the 4th brought on board Captain Hollenstein, of the Forty-second Illinois, and 23 sharpshooters of his command, who volunteered their services, which were gratefully accepted. Colonel Buford remained on board until the last moment to encourage us. I informed the officers and crew of the character of the undertaking, and all expressed a readiness to make the venture. In order to resist boarding parties in case we should be disabled, the sailors were well armed, and pistols, cutlasses, muskets, boarding-pikes and hand grenades were within reach. Hose was attached to the boilers for throwing scalding water over any one who might attempt to board. If it should be found impossible to save the vessel, it was designed to sink rather than burn her, as the loss of life would probably be greater in the latter case by the explosion of her magazine. During the afternoon there was promise of a clear, moonlight night, and it was determined to wait until the moon was down and then make the attempt, whatever the chances. Having gone so far, we could not abandon the project without a bad effect on the men, equal almost to failure.

"At ten o'clock the moon had gone down, and the sky, the earth and the river were alike hidden in the black shadow of a thunderstorm, which had now spread itself over all the heavens. As the time seemed favorable, I ordered the first master to cast off. Dark clouds now rapidly rose over us and enveloped us in almost total darkness, except when the sky was lighted up by the welcome flames of vivid lightning, to show us the perilous way we were to take. Now and then the dim outline of the landscape could be seen, and the forest bending under the roaring storm that came rushing up the river.

"With our bow pointing to the island we passed the lowest point of land without being observed, it appears, by the enemy. All speed was given to the vessel to drive her through the tempest. The flashes of lightning continued with frightful brilliancy and 'almost every second,' wrote a correspondent, 'every brace, post and outline could be seen with startling distinctness, enshrouded by a bluish white glare of light, and then her form for the next minute would become merged in the intense darkness.' When opposite Battery No. 2, on the mainland, the smokestack blazed up, but the fire was soon subdued. It was caused by the soot becoming dry, as the escape of steam, which usually kept the stacks wet, had been sent to the wheel-house, as already mentioned, to prevent noise. With such vivid lightning as prevailed during the whole passage, there was no prospect of escaping the vigilance of the enemy, but there was good reason to hope that he would be unable to point his guns accurately. Again the smokestacks took fire, and were soon put out ; and then the roar of the enemy's guns began, and from Batteries Nos. 2, 3 and 4 came almost incessantly the sharp crack and screaming sound of their rifle shells, which seemed to unite with the electric batteries of the clouds to annihilate us.

"While nearing the island, or some shoal point, during a few minutes of total darkness, we were startled by the loud, sharp order, 'Hard a-port,' from our brave and skillful pilot, First Master Hoel. We almost grazed the island, and, it appears, were not observed through the storm until we were close in- and the enemy, having no time to point his guns, fired at random. In fact, we ran so near that the enemy did not, probably could not, depress his guns sufficiently. While close under the lee of the island, and during a lull in the storm and in the firing, one of our pilots heard a Confederate officer shout, 'Elevate your guns !' 'Yes, confound you,' said the pilot, in a much lower key, 'elevate.' It is probable that the muzzles of those guns had been depressed to keep the rain out of them, and the officers, not expecting another night attack in such a storm, and arriving late, ordered the guns elevated just in time to save us from the direct fire of the enemy's heaviest fort; and this, no doubt, was the cause of our remarkable escape. Nearly all the enemy's shot went over us.

"Having passed the principal batteries, we were greatly relieved from suspense, patiently endured, however, by the officers and crew. But there was another formidable obstacle in the way—a floating battery, which was the great 'war elephant' of the Confederates, built to blockade the Mississippi permanently. As we passed her she fired six or eight shots at us, but without effect. One ball struck the coal barge, and one was found in a bale of hay; we found also one or two musket-bullets. We arrived at New Madrid about midnight with no one hurt, and were most joyfully received by our army. At the suggestion of Paymaster Nixon all hands 'spliced the main-brace.'"

How a Sixteen-year-old Boy Made General Grant Obey His Own Orders.—Captain John R. Steere, now an inmate of the Soldiers' Home, tells a good story, showing how he, when but sixteen years of age, made General Grant obey his own orders.

The occurrence took place in the early stages of the war, shortly after Grant had received his commission as brigadier-general, and was placed in command of the military district of Missouri, with headquarters at Cairo. John Steere, then a boy a little over sixteen years of age, enlisted and was ordered, with others, to report at Cairo, which they did. Five days after enlisting they were drilled in marching and manœuvring without uniform or arms. This was continued for a few days, when the new recruits got a uniform and an old Harper's Ferry musket, one of those old affairs that every time the gun was discharged the shooter had to go hunting for the hammer of his gun.

The morning after young Steere got his gun he was stationed at General Grant's headquarters as guard. The headquarters was located on the levee fronting the Ohio River, near the junction with the Mississippi River. It was in November, and the day was a cold and boisterous one. Steere's military experience was very limited indeed, and the inclement weather did not exactly suit him. His orders were to let no one except an officer, or one on official business, enter the building. He stood at his post of duty until chilled through and through, when he set his musket up in one corner of the door, leaning against the sill, and himself close up against the building, with the cape of his overcoat pulled up over his ears to keep warm.

As every person who came near the place seemed to be an officer, he molested no one, devoting all his time and attention to keeping himself warm and comfortable. Morpheus courted him, and he was on the verge of taking a pleasant snooze when some one coming down the stairway aroused him. Looking up he saw an officer buckling on an elegant sword. After passing through the door the officer came to a halt, and, looking at the guard indignantly, asked :

"What are you doing there?"

"I'm the guard," replied Steere.

"An excellent guard indeed. Do you know whose headquarters this is?"

"Yes, sir ; General Grant's."

The officer looked at the guard a moment in silence, and then thundered :

"Stand up there, sir, and bring your gun to a shoulder!"

Young Steere did as requested, bringing his gun to a shoulder like a squirrel hunter. The officer took the gun from him and went through the manual of arms for him. He remained with him for fifteen or twenty minutes, until he taught him how to handle his gun, when he asked :

"How long have you been in the service?"

"Several days."

"Do you know who I am?"

"No, sir ; never saw you before."

"I am General Grant. You have deserted your post of duty, sir, which is a very serious breach of discipline. I will not punish you this time, but, young man, be very careful it does not occur again. Orders must be strictly and promptly obeyed always."

Several days after this young Steere was put on guard on a steamboat which was being loaded with provisions and ammunition, with orders to allow no one with a lighted pipe or cigar to come within a given distance—about fifty feet. He had not been at his post of duty more than an hour when General Grant approached with a lighted cigar between his teeth. He seemed to be deep in thought, but the moment he came near the gang-plank his musings were interrupted.

"Halt!" cried the young guard, bringing his gun to his shoulder.

The General was taken completely by surprise. He looked at the young guard, who had him covered with his gun, amazed, and then his countenance showed traces of rising anger. But he did not budge an inch.

"I have been taught to obey orders strictly and promptly," explained Steere, quoting the General; "and as my orders are to allow no one to approach this boat with a lighted cigar, you will please throw yours away."

Grant smiled, threw his cigar into the river, and crossed the gang-plank on to the boat.

An Explosive Convoy.—We started for Vicksburg, writes ex-Paymaster Pearson, in company with the *Jacob Strader*, the largest steamboat on the lower river. The *Strader* was burdened with thousands of tons of powder and fixed ammunition for the army. Together we formed, perhaps, the most explosive convoy that ever sailed the Mississippi. The holds were crammed with powder and percussion shell; powder was piled on the main decks aft the furnaces and covered with tarpaulins to keep out the sparks. Lower and upper guards and cabins were stacked with cartridges for small arms.

As we glided down stream Captain Birch called me to the upper deck and introduced me to the queerest looking "infernal machine" we had yet encountered. Belligerent cranks were constantly bringing to the naval authorities some new invention for destruction of the human species "to be tried." As for four years the Confederate States furnished subjects for these experiments, they should be entitled to a bill in equity against the inventors for a share of the profits.

This thing placed in charge of Captain Birch was a sort of infantry platoon on wheels—a rank of rifle barrels ranged parallel and mounted like a boat howitzer. By percussion the whole platoon was simultaneously discharged in "one time and one motion." Birch told me he had reason to fear that the Confederates were aware of the coming of our convoy, and that somewhere on the route to Vicksburg they might waylay us and try to blow us up. In case opportunity offered, he wished me to take charge of the "infernal machine" and report upon its capabilities. We charged the "platoon" and blazed away over the river a few times to get elevation and range; then loaded and left it ready for emergency.

Next morning about 7 o'clock, as we were steaming down the river, I had just rolled over for another snooze, when I was aroused by a crash through the sides of the ship, together with a rattling report of light artillery. In a moment came a kick at my door, with the words: "Hallo! Get up! We're in a fight!" I bounced out, and being ready harnessed, excepting coat and boots, ran for the hurricane deck and the "infernal machine." We were passing through "Cypress Bend," and things around looked interesting.

On shore, abreast the narrowest of the channel, was a four-gun battery of field pieces, manned by about 200 Confederates, all peppering away like a Fourth of July. About 100 yards ahead was the *Strader*. She had been the target of the first volley and escaped damage. The *General Lyon* came next, and here the enemy had better luck, putting all four of the shot of their second volley through us. It is scarcely necessary to mention that our cargo was unscathed. Had any part of it been struck, this chapter would have been written by somebody else.

Next after the *Lyon* came the transport *New Kentucky*, loaded with troops and mules. The third round of the battery blew her up. She drifted and lodged upon a sand-bar and lay there helpless, enveloped in a cloud of steam, while the battery poured shot into her as fast as the guns could be served. The men not busy with the field-pieces amused themselves with small arms. Many were perched in the small trees astraddle of the limbs, whence they kept up a lively shower of buckshot and little bullets. But they fired too high.

Alongside our lee was the gunboat *Signal*. Captain Birch suggested that she engage the battery and rescue the disabled transport, which was being roughly treated. The commander of the *Signal* objected that, being a "tin-clad," he could not go within range without endangering his own boilers.

"If you won't do it," said Birch, "I will!"

We rounded to and went for the battery. The long thirty-two-pounder on the forecastle was in charge of an old man-of-war's-man and gunner, Acting Ensign John Powell. As we neared the Confederates he sent a shell which struck in the river bank beneath them. Another quickly followed and burst in the midst of the convocation around the guns. It caused a "scatterment," and they began to limber up.

Meanwhile the "infernal machine" was tested. Aimed into the tree tops, it fired a whole platoon. I had squatted down behind it to aim, and, intent on the effect of the discharge, forgot to keep clear of the recoil. I picked myself up with a sore head, for which I was compensated by witnessing the comical style in which the occupants of the tree-tops tumbled out. It reminded me of old-time blackbird shooting. The platoon was again got into line of battle and fired another blizzard with good effect, while the old thirty-two pounder put in some more notices to quit, so persuasive that our foes were soon in full retreat across the bend, affectionately followed by our kind adieux so long as we could see them.

The steamer *New Kentucky* was rescued and taken in tow. It then behooved us to hasten on and pass the other side of the bend before the battery reached it to intercept us. Since we had force enough, it would, perhaps, have been better and safer to have landed and captured the guns than to risk their bad marksmanship again. Fortunately we got ahead of them and escaped a repetition of their attentions.

One of the party of hostiles was subsequently captured, and from him we learned that the shell so appositely planted among them from the *Lyon* killed and wounded sixteen men of the battery. To how much credit the "infernal machine" was entitled is uncertain. Judging by the energy with which it kicked over its engineer, it ought to have slaughtered all there was left.

Our loss was trifling, our escape miraculous. Of the shots which struck the *Lyon*, two passed through the flues close in front, the others just behind her boilers. One actually knocked off the button of the steam gauge. A divergence of one inch either way would have been destruction to the entire convoy. It seemed as if Providence had purposed an example of "upon what slender threads hang everlasting things." The loss of those cargoes of ammunition might have materially changed results at Vicksburg. Had our assailants succeeded in blowing us up it would have been a rich joke on themselves. We were not thirty yards distant when they struck us, and had we "gone off" there would not have been a grease spot left of them.

Grant's Pie Joke.—This story purports to be told by an officer of General Grant's staff, and refers to a time in 1861 when he was sent with a brigade to southern Mississippi to repel a threatened invasion by Jeff Thompson. The country through which the troops passed was chiefly a wilderness in which not a hog, a chicken or an ear of corn was to be captured by the boys. Finally Lieutenant Wickfield, of an Indiana cavalry regiment, with an advance guard of eight mounted men, came across a farmhouse. He halted his command, and, with two second lieutenants, entered, represented himself to be General Grant, and demanded dinner. The General's name had already acquired some fame in that region, and the family scurried about and set forth what they had, loudly professing their loyalty. The lieutenants ate all they could and departed, after the family had refused to take any pay for what had been furnished. Later in the day it happened that General Grant himself stopped in front of the same house and asked if he could be given a meal, but was told that General Grant and his staff had been there and eaten everything in the house but one pumpkin pie. After learning that the family name was Selvidge and leaving half a dollar to insure their keeping the pie until he should send an officer for it, the General rode off. That night, greatly to the surprise of the troops, after a camping ground had been selected, the whole force was ordered to turn out for parade. Something of great importance was supposed to be about to happen, when the Assistant Adjutant-General read in a loud voice before the lines that had been drawn up, the following order:

HEADQUARTERS ARMY IN THE FIELD.
Special Order No. ——.
Lieutenant Wickfield, of the Indiana cavalry, having eaten everything in Mrs. Selvidge's house, at the crossing of the Trenton and Pocahontas and

Black River and Cape Girardeau roads, except one pumpkin pie, Lieutenant Wickfield is hereby ordered to return with an escort of 100 cavalry and eat that pie also.
U. S. GRANT,
Brigadier-General Commanding.

The troops were then dismissed in a state of bewilderment, but by the time the lieutenant was ready to leave camp with his escort to perform his singular duty, the joke was appreciated, and he was followed by peals of laughter.

Mrs. Howe's Battle Hymn.—The greatest poem of the war was written at Washington by Julia Ward Howe, under the title of "The Battle Hymn of the Republic." It is sung to the tune of "John Brown," and commences, "Mine eyes have seen the glory of the coming of the Lord." Mrs. Howe wrote it early one morning, and it is said she penned it with her eyes shut. The night before she had been out riding in the country near Washington and her party had narrowly escaped being captured by a troop of Confederates. As they came into Washington they sang "John Brown's Body," and the tune kept ringing in Mrs. Howe's head all night. When she awoke before daylight she began to make verses to it, and in the fear that she would forget them she wrote them off, according to a habit she had formed to save her eyes, without looking at the paper. Mrs. Howe is still living and she ranks among the leaders of the woman's rights movement. Speaking of "John Brown's Body," the tune itself is an old Methodist camp-meeting tune and the words were adapted to it by a glee club of Boston in 1861. It was first published at Charlestown, Mass. Captain James Greenleaf, an organist of the Harvard Church, set the notes for music and a Massachusetts regiment made them first noted by singing them at Fort Warren in 1861

One of Blackburn's Stories.—Blackburn, writes a newspaper correspondent, was sitting the other night in Chamberlain's with a party of fellow Congressmen when the conversation turned to the war. "Did I ever tell you," he asked, "a funny thing that happened to me during the war? Well, it was in this way: Four days before I went to the front with my regiment we had a little girl baby. She is now grown, and you always see her with me at any social gathering. Well, in our army the furloughs came very rarely. When we got into line there was no great chance for a man to get home. It was about three years afterward that a few of us were one night going down the Mississippi on a river steamer. I had been sick and was returning to my command, but pretty well broken up even then. As for money, we did not have any, and the night was hot, as I lay down on the deck, my throat almost parched with dust. Pretty soon a little girl came along with a big glass of lemonade. I tell you it looked good to me. She saw me eyeing it, stopped a minute, looked doubtfully at me, and finally came to my side. 'You look as if you wanted something to drink,' she said, and offered me the glass. It wasn't quite the square thing to do, but I took it and handed it back to her empty. It was like nectar to me. Then I thanked the little creature and sent her away. Soon after, just like every child, she came back leading her mother to the poor soldier. By Jupiter, it was my wife, and the girl was the baby whom I had last seen as a baby but just born. You can imagine the reunion. They were with my brother's family and happened to be going down the river. That was the only time during the four years' fighting that I saw my wife and baby, and under these circumstances what man would ever forget it?"

An Incident at Shiloh.—Major W. H. Chamberlin was an officer of the Eighty-first Ohio Volunteer Infantry, and served with General Grant during the whole of the campaign of 1862. Major Chamberlin tells a story of the General which has a peculiar significance in that it gives a key to his mode of action. "It was on the second day of the battle of Shiloh," said the Major in speaking of the circumstance. "The first day, you know, had been disastrous to our forces, which had been driven back. Early in the morning of the second day General Grant rode through our lines to the front, accompanied by some officer, I do not know who. The two were having an animated conversation, and as they passed where I was standing I heard

General Grant remark : 'All the advantage is on the side of
the attacking party.' Within a few minutes after they had
passed me I heard the guns on our right open up, an order
to advance was given, and the Union soldiers, who were compelled to retire on the previous day, themselves assumed the
aggressive and were victorious. That one remark of General
Grant was significant of his whole career. He believed in
attack rather than defense, and Shiloh alone proved the cor-
rectness of his theory."

Grant's Appreciation of Sheridan.—In 1875 Grant attended
a centennial celebration at Concord, Mass., and on his return
to New York three gentlemen rode in his company in a com-
partment of a drawing-room car, and during the ride he occupied the greater portion of the time in conversation, greatly to
the surprise of one or two of his companions, who had accepted
his usual reticence as a common and uniform habit. But he
went on in this talk and spoke of himself, modestly, and of the
way in which the responsibilities of the war grew upon him.
He felt them much less than might naturally be supposed. He
had relief and great help in his always trustworthy chief military subordinates, of whom he spoke in terms of the highest
praise. Referring to several of them by name, and especially
to Sherman, for whom he bore a strong personal affection, and
to Sheridan, he said with emphasis: "I consider Phil Sheridan
the greatest captain of the age!" And, as if to show how complete his confidence in him was, it being impossible for him to
show his own estimate by any ordinary manner of speech, he
used this striking and extravagant illustration: "If Sheridan
had been in Von Moltke's place in the Franco-Prussian war, he
could have dictated terms to the French army without moving
on the French border and without leaving Berlin."

The General's Coffee-Pot.—General M—— was a good
officer. His division of infantry was kept well in hand in camp
and on the pitched field. Rail-stealing was a bucking offense,
and straggling in the presence of the enemy well nigh a capital

one. The consequence was that method and promptness characterized all his subordinates, and, from posting a sentinel to mustering on the battle front, there were celerity and precision. Perhaps the best organized corps under the despot was his household body of detailed servants. But above all these towered high in authority Jim, the major-domo of the military family.

One moonlit evening, two days before Lee's surrender, General M—— was informed by Jim that some supper could be gotten at a house near by. For three days the wagons had not been up, and the General was anxious about them.

"Jim," said he, as we swept along through the country, now and then pausing to pick our way across a gully, "how about the wagons?"

"The wagons, sur, is all rite," said Jim, rather hesitatingly.

"How about the horse team?" said the General.

"Jes' leff it, sur, safe an' soun'," was the reply.

"And the mule team? My English coffee-pot is in that, you know."

"Yes," said Jim, "I know. Pretty rough times for it, too. 'Twas packed in a hurry, and—"

"What!" said the General, suddenly halting. "You don't mean to say that anything has happened to my coffee-pot? Why, I wouldn't take a mint of money for it!"

"Oh, no," replied Jim, "it's all right; only I'm afraid it's got ramjammed a little."

"Ramjammed? Thunder and lightning! Who dared to ramjam my coffee-pot?" roared the major-general.

"I dunno who's dun it," said Jim, tremblingly.

"You'd better know," said the General, as he rode forward. If there was one man rejoiced at Lee's surrender, it was Jim, for, like everything else of value, the coffee-pot disappeared at Appomattox.

Why Grant Did Not Take Lee's Sword.—The Rev. Dr. C. C. McCabe, recently gave this contribution to the war memories connected with the ex-President's name: "A short time ago I had an interview with General Grant. The conversation turned upon the war. I asked him the question, 'Did you take Lee's sword at Appomattox?' His reply was in the following language, almost to the letter: 'No, I did not. Lee came there wearing the magnificent sword which the State of Virginia gave him, evidently expecting that it would be preserved in the archives of the Government. But I did not want him to surrender it to me. I sat down at once and busied myself with writing the terms of surrender. When I had finished them I handed them to General Lee. He read them and remarked: 'They certainly are very generous terms indeed.' He then told me that his cavalrymen owned their own horses, and if they were deprived of them they could not put in their crops. Then I gave the order: 'Take your horses home with you, for you'll need them in the spring ploughing.' This is the simple story of the surrender, told to me in Grant's own parlor. Cæsar would have had that sword; Napoleon would have demanded it; Wellington would not have been satisfied without it; but U. S. Grant was too great to take it."

An Anecdote of Stanton.—About the close of the war a number of persons who had been employed in the carpenter's shop of the Quartermaster-General's Department were indicted for using government lumber for private purposes. One of them was a case of peculiar hardship, as the prosecution was inspired by malice. The criminal docket was crowded, and the party who was on bail stood but little chance of a speedy trial. He could get no employment and could not leave the city. As a last resort, it was determined that an appeal should be made to Mr. Stanton, and the writer of this being junior counsel, was selected to intercede with the great War Secretary. I remember very well with what a heavy foot I started to the War Department. On the way I procured a note of introduction from Colonel Moore, then at the White House. I entered through the room of General Pelouze, and was by that officer introduced to Mr. Stanton, who stood behind his high desk, with his large spectacles and huge beard making him appear the image of defiance. As soon as I was introduced he came around and grasped my hand and said he was glad to see me, and politely asked me what he could do for me. I stated the case to him. He said: "That matter has passed beyond my control, and is now in the hands of the law officers." I said: "Well, Mr. Stanton, have you any objection to the prosecution being dropped?" "No," he said, "none in the world." Emboldened by this, I said: "Have you any objection to saying that on paper?" He looked thoughtful for a moment, and then said: "I will not put anything on paper, because the District-Attorney might think I was interfering with his affairs; but you may say to that officer that any course he may pursue will be satisfactory to me." That was the only time I ever came in contact with Mr. Stanton while he was Secretary of War, and when I got outside I felt almost stunned at the kind and cordial reception he gave me

General Kilpatrick and His Old Lady Friend.—The following is a story which the late General Judson Kilpatrick used to relate at his own expense: Soon after the announcement in the newspapers that he had been appointed Minister to Chili, General Kilpatrick was met by an old lady who had known him from childhood, and to whose bucolic mind the General's large way of stating things had sometimes seemed like exaggeration. "Wall, Jud," she said, "I hear you have been called to the ministry. Glad to hear it. You'll make a real good preacher; but (solemnly), Jud, you must stop your lyin'"

Recollections of General Grant.—Colonel William H. Paine, assistant engineer of the Brooklyn bridge, served continuously on the staff of the Generals of the Army of the Potomac, his chief business being to prepare the maps of the country through which the army was moving. While General Meade was his commander he had several opportunities to see much of Grant and study his characteristics. Colonel Paine relates the following incident: "Immediately after crossing the Rapidan, the first movement of the Wilderness campaign under Grant, the enemy struck our extreme right and gained an advantage.

General Shaler was captured, and if the enemy had only known it, there was a way open to advance to headquarters, our line being broken on the side. I reported this state of affairs to Meade in the presence of General Grant. Some of us were much agitated. This is the conversation that occurred between Grant and Meade as I remember it:

"Meade—'In these circumstances the throwing up of earthworks would seem to be the best course to pursue. In this way we can protect the army.'

"Grant—'We will move forward in the morning.'

"Meade—'But the enemy will be in our immediate front.'

"Grant—'Then flank them.'

"Meade—'What disposition of the troops must be made for that movement?'

"Grant—'You are in command of this part of the army, and will fight better on your own plans than mine.'

"This will illustrate one of Grant's characteristics—the manner in which he trusted his subordinates. He placed implicit confidence in them, and although he sometimes made mistakes, his judgment was generally excellent in the selection of those who were to serve him. He was not in the habit of going into details; he gave his general orders in few words. As to his courage on the most trying occasion there could be no question. While the movement across Hatcher's Run was in progress, Grant rode out of the woods followed by his staff, and, having reached a point in advance of the main line, and slightly in the rear of the skirmish line, he dismounted and sat down under a tree. He called for a map which I had prepared, and, with a lighted cigar in his mouth, he examined it in the coolest possible manner. The enemy were at this time making a target of him and his staff at a moderate range. But Grant remained quietly seated for a quarter of an hour, entirely undisturbed by the bursting of shells in his immediate vicinity. There were several old soldiers there who thought it was the hottest spot they had ever struck in their lives. When Grant remounted and rode off, there was no haste in his movements. Under all circumstances he had full possession of his faculties and judgment. His words were few. He hardly ever displayed any humor when in the army. A smile from him was more than a loud laugh from others. I often looked at him and wondered if he comprehended all that was going on. I am convinced that he did, and that he brought his best judgment to bear in weighing every matter presented for his consideration. He would not leave anything to doubt. He would never change his plans until there was a positive demand for a change. He had implicit confidence in those he put in charge of movements, and would support them. Stolid as Grant appeared to be, I have no doubt th .t he felt as deeply about the horrors of war as those who were more demonstrative."

The Great War Secretary.—Speaking of Stanton, writes a newspaper correspondent, reminds me of an old stager here at the capital who undertook to desciibe to me the Secretary's daily routine in war times. There was then, as now, a good deal of messengering and card-taking at the doors of department secretaries, but access to S anton was always possible to people who knew how to wait. His office would be crowded every morning when he took his seat. To the first visitor who stepped up he would say brusquely, his eyes gleaming through his glasses like fixed bayonets :

"What do you want?"

"Mr. Secretary," said the petitioner, a tall, sinewy Westerner, "our folks have had a fair, and filled thirty-seven boxes of good things for the boys in our —— Illinois regiment. I want transportation—" etc., etc.

"Don't bother me with that. Here!" And the Secretary would dash his pen on a bit of paper, give it to the tall man, and dismiss him.

"What is it?" This to an Irish woman.

"Plaze, sor, an' I want to see me husband in Fort Myer."

"You can't. Next."

"I wanted to ask—" this time it is a New York merchant, shrewd, smooth and calculating—" about the post tradership at ——. Is there to be a change, and has any one been given that post?"

"No, sir; and you can't have it for yourself or anybody else."

"I want that;" and a thick-set, quick-motioned man threw down a piece of paper.

"All right. Next!"

The next would, perhaps, say not a word, but stick a paper under Stanton's nose:

"Yes; go to Townsend, Adjutant-General. It's none of my business."

A brigadier-general stepped up:

"What are you here for?"

"I thought I would look in, Mr. Secretary, and see—"

"That's enough, sir. Don't let me see or hear of you in Washington again for six months. If you do I'll jail you, as sure as you live."

A slim, brown-faced lieutenant stepped up:

"I have a friend, Mr. Secretary, in the One Hundred and Fourteenth New York, that I want to get transferred to my regiment and company. He is my best friend. Can it be done?"

"My dear fellow, it can't. I should like to please a good-looking boy like you; but if I did it would break up the discipline of the whole army in ninety days. You are well. Just from the front? Good-bye. God bless you."

Such was the great War Secretary.

A Sharpshooter's Story.—In the spring of 1864 General Crook's Division, of which I was a member, was ordered to strike tents and leave the great Kanawha Valley to join General Hunter's army in his campaign down the Shenandoah Valley to Lynchburg. A few weeks later we were near Staunton, enjoying a brisk skirmish with the enemy. From that time on I was duly assigned to the position of scout and sharpshooter, and found my post of duty in the extreme skirmish line, where I could peck at the Southerners at my will, and without being molested in my work by some over-knowing officer in charge, who simply wanted to say something so as to fully assert his authority. My position suited me to a T, and Colonel Comly was only too well aware of the fact that he had made no mistake in selecting me for the position.

I remember the skirmish before Staunton. I recall how I chased a "reb" through fields and over fences for two miles, and how at last he sought refuge inside of a little stone milk-house right close to the main pike; how, as I was climbing a seven-rail fence to get at the fellow, my heavy knapsack over-balanced my little, frail body and down I tumbled—head first; how the "reb," peeping through the open door, saw the sad fix I was in, but instead of sticking his bayonet into me, as I expected he would, took to his heels once more and skedaddled clear out of sight and reach.

I was in the skirmish before Staunton, where the bullets scratched off the bark of every tree that I saw fit to dodge behind, and I became convinced that some individual "reb" had a special purpose in taking my life. But who could be the man? and what could be his object in selecting me for his victim? I watched for him high and low, but failed to discover his whereabouts, though all the while the bullets of the mysterious rifleman were playing merry havoc with my fears. I was used to having bullets fly near me, but they came at random, for in the heat of battle bullets fly for no man; only they who by chance stand in the way direct are made to feel the kiss of the stinging lead

But I discovered my man at last. My eyes descried the smoke of a gun some two hundred yards to the right of my front, and I had just time to dodge behind my tree when a bullet came whizzing by, knocking off a piece of bark within a few inches of my face. Then as I looked out to see who it was shooting at me, I discovered a tall, heavy-set man, wearing a big slouch hat, sneaking from behind a tree to open on me again, and he did. He fired at me again and again, and every time the bullets skinned the bark off the very trees behind which I sought shelter. After the skirmish was over I told some of my comrades of the sharpshooter who took such interest in picking me out during the afternoon for his especial enjoyment, but the boys only laughed at my expense and said that I merely imagined it to be so—that no sharpshooter was such a fool as to waste his powder on a boy of my diminutive form.

The next day we advanced on Lexington, and before we had made much progress on our journey the enemy opened a pretty lively skirmish with us. We had no more than fairly got started in the affray before I became convinced of the fact that I was being marked by some particular man, as certain shots came in a manner that meant business. Imagine my feelings when, in looking over the ground in front, I discovered the man with the white slouch hat standing between two trees, coolly firing away at me. I do not know why it was, but in that moment there crept an awful terror over my soul, as I realized that I was marked and that a human being was actually thirsting for my life's blood. But the more uneasy I felt over the terrible discovery, the more determined I became to make things as hot as possible before the mysterious man with the white slouch hat got his work in on me. From that time on I became marvelously reckless and desperate. I felt that my life was doomed—that it was a question of a few days ere I would be called away, and that I might as well make my life glorious during its brief earthly existence. I entered the conflict with a renewed vigor, with a deeper and bitterer vim. I loaded my gun and fired with a quickness that was surprising, and my aim seemed to be far more effective than ever before. My fellow skirmishers noted the sudden change that had come over me, though I did not see fit to explain matters, but went right on, rushing into danger and what seemed certain death at every given opportunity.

We reached Lexington that night after having enjoyed a spirited skirmish all through the afternoon. The following morning found us on the road to Lynchburg at an early hour. But we had not gone far on our way before the enemy opened on us and a hot skirmish followed. I was on the extreme line of advance and the man on my right was a particular chum of mine, John Black, who by the way was only nineteen years old (three years my senior), but a perfect dare-devil of a soldier. After we had been skirmishing about an hour Black yelled out to me :

"Say, Jeff!"

"Well, what?"

"Do you see that tall 'son-of-a-gun of a reb,' with a big white hat, pecking away at us?"

"No; where is he?"

"Do you see that apple tree in the little field just this side of yonder wood?"

"Yes!"

"Well, you just keep an eye open in that direction and you'll soon see the cuss."

The next moment I saw a man step from behind the tree I was watching; then I saw the smoke of his gun, and before the report of the shot reached my ears a missile of lead whizzed by, passing within a foot of my head. It was the man with the white slouch hat.

Then there came a lull over the scene. The fight rather subsided for a few moments or so, only, however, to be renewed with a livelier vigor; but during the lull Black and I got behind the same tree and held a confidential chat. I related my adventures of the past two days, how I tumbled on the man with the white slouch hat and how he had paid especial attention to me during the time and was still attentive to me. Black was amazed. Who could this devil with the white slouch hat be, and why had he picked on a mere boy like me for his victim? "It's a bad piece of business," said he, in a serious tone, "and I can't for the life of me understand it. It is evidently plain that he has marked you as his own, and that as long as he can find you he is going to shoot at you."

Black thought it would be advisable, under the circumstances, for me to quit the skirmish line and return to the main body of the army, but I laughed at the idea and expressed the determination to stick to the skirmish line while life lasted, in spite of the man with the white slouch hat. "Then," said Black, "let's stick closely together, and whenever one of us corners the 'son-of-a-gun,' we'll both join in to make it most interestingly hot for him."

The next day was a fearfully warm one all around. General Hunter had fooled his opportunities away until the foe had ample time to be reinforced from the army about Richmond and Petersburg. The result was, we failed to capture Lynchburg. Daylight had no sooner made its appearance before the advance guard of the Confederate army opened fire on us. In a moment our rear was protected by a line of skirmishers, with Black and myself at our favorite post of duty, and the very first Southerner that my eyes fell on was no other than the man with the white slouch hat. I pointed him out to Black and then we fired at the fellow with vehemence, but with the usual effect. He, in return, devoted his sole attention to me, never bothering Black, though we were only some twenty feet apart. The enemy's advance line pushed us closely and hotly all day long, and when darkness came both Black and I felt a brief relief, as it at least gave us an opportunity to eat a morsel of dough—the only article of food left us. Our forces kept up the retreat all through the night. Fences were burned along the roadway so as to keep the men wide awake and in line, yet in spite of this precaution men here and there, completely played out from over-work and hunger, would drop out of the line, only to be taken as prisoners by the Confederates, who followed dangerously close at our heels.

Daylight had hardly set in before the enemy opened on our rear. Again the skirmishers were let loose to hold them at bay while the main body of our troops marched on in quick retreat. It was near 9 o'clock before either Black or I caught sight of our man, but we discovered him at last. We found him in our near front pecking away at me for dear life.

"Let's try and get better acquainted with him," said Black.

"How?" I asked.

"Let's try to pick up a handkerchief flirtation with him;" and with the words Black pulled out a white handkerchief and waved it in the air. But he answered him only with a bullet.

"Suppose you try him, Jeff."

"All right." And out went my handkerchief to the breeze.

"Hello! he recognizes you," exclaimed Black.

Sure enough, the fellow was standing out from behind his tree waving a red handkerchief in answer to my signal.

"The son-of-a-gun !" exclaimed Black. "He wouldn't notice me, but I will notice him all the same ;" and as he spoke he brought up his rifle and fired at our man, who was still standing a few feet from his tree, signaling to me with wild delight. But Black missed, as usual, though the shot brought the fellow to time, as he quickly dodged behind his tree.

Just before sunset there came a brief lull over the scene of action. We had reached a piece of natural fortified ground, and our commander-in-chief concluded it best to show fight, so as to give the trains and heavy artillery a chance to get out of reach of the enemy. The main body of our troops lay in ambush behind a long ridge of ground. The enemy was advancing slowly and steadily just on the other side of the ridge. It was found necessary to display two or three skirmishers on the top of the ridge, so as to watch the movements of the enemy. But the top of the ridge was a mighty risky position for any one, as there were only three trees within a distance of a hundred rods, and not one of these was over a foot in diameter. This was rather thin shelter for a boy in blue, within the reach of some ten thousand guns. But Colonel Comly called for two volunteers to climb the ridge and watch the enemy, and the call was hardly made before Black and I were on our feet, and a moment later we were on the top of the ridge. We found the sharpshooters just below us, within a hundred rods, and just beyond them the enemy were moving through field and wood. It was a glorious sight. But somehow it did not seem so glorious when fifty or more of the sharpshooters below us opened fire. The way we hugged those apple trees was a caution, and the way the bullets played on the trees was anything but agreeable. It was close quarters—too close even for such reckless dare-devils as we had the reputation of being. Just as sure as one of us stepped from behind his respective tree to fire, the very air would be resonant with bullets.

We had held our positions some twenty minutes, expecting every moment to get a dose of lead, when all of a sudden the sharpshooters let up on us. Just then we caught sight of the man with the white slouch hat. He was standing by a small bush in a small ploughed field just beyond the foot of the ridge. The fellow was all alone, and evidently in a good humor, for no sooner did he see that he was recognized by us than he flung his handkerchief to the breeze and waved it wildly. In a trice our handkerchiefs were out, and we set up a wild cheer that surprised our comrades behind us, who were in the dark as to the fun we were enjoying. But the line of Confederate sharpshooters stationed at the foot of the ridge took in the whole scene, and seemed to understand the affair between us. Not a shot greeted us when Black raised his rifle and fired at our man. But the smoke of his gun had not time to clear away when the report of a gun in our front was heard, and at the same time Black was struck by a missile of lead and mortally hurt. Just then a shrill yell greeted our ears, and at the same time a bullet swept past in front of my eyes. I looked up, but my evil spirit was not to be seen. I only caught a glimpse of a bit of smoke rising in the air, just above the bush where but a moment before I had seen the man I was after.

"He must be hid behind that bush," groaned Black.

"I'll soon find out," said I, and raising my rifle I sent a bullet in the direction of the bush. There came a yell, and then we saw a man step from behind the bush I had shot at, stagger a few steps back, and then fall to the ground. I had killed the man without learning the secret of his enmity.

On to Richmond.—It was in April, 1865, writes Mr. Elisha N. Pierce, that I was attached to the *Commodore Perry*, under Captain Foster, lying on the James River about half a mile above the Dutch Gap canal. The lines surrounding Lee's army were being drawn tighter and closer and the final blow was about to be struck. On that morning it was my watch on deck. About 4 o'clock Captain Foster, who had been taking an hour's rest, came up from his cabin and asked me if I had heard any firing up the river during his absence. I told him that I had not. He thought in silence a moment and said, "Mr. Pierce, I would not be surprised if the end of all this would come within the next twenty-four hours." Scarcely had he spoken when a sheet of flame shot into the air, followed by a tremendous explosion.

"There," exclaimed the captain, "goes a rebel iron-clad." Two similar explosions followed immediately. After waiting for further developments Captain Foster ordered his gig away, and, going ashore, climbed to the top of the "Old Crow Nest" signal tower, from which an excellent view could be obtained for miles around. In about an hour the captain returned on board, and in a few minutes the flag ship signaled the *Perry*, "Get under way. Take the lead to Richmond. Be very careful of torpedoes."

The old boat had borne the brunt of several severe fights, and that she was now going to attempt to clear the James River of torpedoes, made the officers and crew hope that they would be the first to reach Richmond. The boatswain's whistle called all hands to weigh anchor, and in a very short time the *Perry* commenced to move up the river. Boats were sent out in advance. As the old ship made progress up the stream, a little chip was seen floating on the water. It was a torpedo float. The boat crews went to work cutting lines and wires until the infernal box was brought to the surface, the can cut open and the contents spilled into the river. In this way fifty-one torpedoes were removed and the James opened to navigation.

When the *Perry* reached Fort Darling she ran aground on obstructions placed across the river. Orders were given the chief engineer to pay no attention to the engine bells, but to force the vessel forward and backward as hard as possible until she was worked off. There we were, working away, when the United States steamship *Malvern*, which was Admiral Porter's flagship, came up astern of us. We then learned for the first time that President Lincoln was on board, and had made his arrangements to accompany the fleet to Richmond. It being impossible for the admiral's vessel to go by us, he determined to take the President to Richmond in his barge. The boat was lowered, the President and admiral taking seats in the stern-sheets, while Lieutenant Barnes, with a body guard of marines, followed in the *Malvern's* first cutter.

Between the *Perry* and the shore was a very narrow channel

of deep water, through which the admiral intended the boats to pass. The place, however, was found too narrow to use the oars, and so, backing water a little, the crew pulled hard, thinking by the power thus obtained the boat would pass through. The admiral did not take into account the current, however, and those in the boat were surprised to find themselves drifting in the direction of the steamer's immense wheel. Just at this moment the engineer turned the lever, and in a moment the engines were churning up the water, to the alarm of the boat's crew.

The President shouted "Stop her!" and the admiral followed suit. The uproar immediately reached the ears of Captain Foster, who with one bound reached the engine-room hatch and shouted to the engineer to reverse. In a moment this was done and the boat was safe. When the barge had backed out of her perilous situation the admiral, rising and blowing the water out of his mouth, called out: "Where is the captain of the vessel?"

"Here I am," said Captain Foster, leaning over the ship rail.

"Well, sir," said the admiral indignantly, "when you back off from here don't you attempt to go to Richmond, but anchor down below and allow the other vessels to go up before you."

Without a moment's hesitation the captain, in his usual tone of voice, responded, "Aye, aye, sir," and in a moment more the boats went on. After working the engine for some time without avail the captain squeezed the three tugs, which he had used in clearing the river, through the channel. A large hawser was then attached to the *Perry* from each of the tugs and the captain gave the order that when he waved his handkerchief the tugs should go ahead at full speed. The handkerchief dropped, the tugs started, and the old *Perry*, putting on steam, crashed through the obstructions, and in a moment more was floating on the broad stream. Continuing the journey under a full head of steam, Richmond was reached, and the *Commodore Perry* was the first ship bearing national colors to drop anchor before the city. A few hours after the *Malvern* hove in sight, and dropped anchor near us.

At evening the admiral, in company with the President, who had passed the afternoon in the rebel capital, returned on board his vessel, and the greatest ordeal of the whole campaign was now before Captain Foster, as he was obliged to go on board the flagship and report the presence of his vessel to the admiral. As he left in the gig his face looked a trifle paler than usual, but his great dark eyes showed determination to face the music like the man that he was. Going on board he was met by Fleet Captain Bruce, who whispered in his ear, "You'll get ----, old fellow, for coming up here." His presence was communicated to the orderly at the cabin door, who announced to the admiral that "Captain Foster had come aboard to report." He was accordingly asked into the cabin, where he saw the President and the admiral seated at a small centre table. Saluting both, Captain Foster said: "Admiral, I have the honor to report the arrival of the United States steamship *Commodore Perry* at Richmond."

The admiral, in a very stern voice, replied: "Captain Foster, I thought I told you not to come up to Richmond."

The captain answered: "Sir, I did not understand you so. I thought you told me that when I backed off not to attempt to come up here."

"Well," returned the admiral in the same stern voice, "what of it?"

In the same measured accents which characterized the whole conversation, the captain answered: "Sir, I did not back off. I ran her over bow first."

The admiral turned all shades of red, but before he could utter an accent "Old Abe" saw the joke and laughingly arose and offered his heartiest congratulations to Captain Foster. The admiral immediately cooled off and, rising, said: "Sir, you can now go on board your vessel. I will see you concerning this matter in the morning." That was the last that ever came of it.

A Chicagoan Tells How His Whisky Made Grant President.—At a private house in Chicago one evening some men were chatting about the vicissitudes of Presidential elections, and the part played by luck in every person's life. An incident as trival as a shower of rain has turned many a victory into a

Waterloo. A fool utters an alliterative sentence and the destiny of a nation is perhaps changed, and history hangs upon a silly phrase. Cleveland's alleged luck was particularly touched upon, and while it was under discussion the host said: "By the way, I sometimes flatter myself that I made Grant President."

The speaker was evidently serious, and as he is an old and well-known merchant in Chicago, there is hardly any reason to doubt the singular story that he told.

"The year the war broke out," he said, "I was a drummer for the old grocery house of Smith & Williams, on Lake street. I frequently visited Mattoon, Ill., and the last time I did so was during that eventful year. The month I forget, but I know it was summer time, for I wore a duster, a curious garment then in vogue, having a cape instead of sleeves and a couple of capacious pockets. I knew the firm of Monroe Bros., at Mattoon, consisting of Frank, James and Bird Monroe. Frank was the senior partner, and managed the business, but the others were lively fellows, and I was accustomed to go on shooting trips with them whenever I visited the town. This time I went to the store as usual, and asked Frank where his brothers were. 'If you want to see them,' was the reply, 'you must go out to the camp. They have joined the army.'

"The camp of the regiment, whose number I forget, was on the outskirts of the town. As I was about to start some one in the grocery store said that the boys would appreciate a little good whisky, as they couldn't get anything of that sort in camp. I walked over to Griffin's bar and got two flat quart flasks of his best liquor, putting one in each pocket. Then off I went. I made my way to the camp all right, and soon ran across my two friends. While we were chatting, I told them what I had in my pockets and asked them where I should unload. 'Come to the Colonel's tent,' said one of them; 'he is an old officer, and he appreciates a drop of something as well as any one.'

"We went to the Colonel's tent, and I was introduced to a red faced, sturdy-looking man who struck me as a typical soldier. He was a man of irascible temper, as I afterward learned but he had done good service in the field, having served with distinction in the Mexican War. Well, we all sat down and began drinking. The time quickly slipped away, and one quart flask was empty. We began on the other. I soon felt that I had taken enough, and that the best thing I could do was to get out of camp and attend to my business. So I said good bye to the boys, and left them.

"That afternoon, I remember, I transacted all my business, and early the next morning was on my way to Chicago. On the train I bought copies of the Chicago papers, and was surprised to see, figuring in black head-lines, the name of my Colonel I read beneath a dispatch dated the night before from Mattoon, Ill., giving an account of serious trouble in the camp that I had visited. It seems that the Colonel became violently drunk, engaged in an altercation with one of his officers, and, drawing his sword, severely wounded the latter. Such an occurrence, of course, made a terrible scandal, and the Colonel was peremptorily discharged from the army.

"At this time U. S. Grant had his hands in his pockets waiting for a job. He had high recommendations to the Governor, and was promised the first vacancy that would occur. The Colonel's discharge made a vacancy for him in the regiment at Mattoon. He took the place and from that day he followed fortune from one victory to another until he entered the White House as President of the nation.

"I met the Monroe boys afterward in Kentucky during the war. I remember one of them said to me then: 'That whisky of yours decided the conduct of this war.' So it did, and perhaps the destiny of the Republic.

"After his discharge the Colonel died from chagrin. He was an experienced and an able soldier. Who knows that but for the incident I have described his name might have figured in the history of the rebellion among the distinguished Northern Generals? And who knows, too, that but for the same incident Grant might have remained in comparative obscurity?"

"True," said a member of the party, getting at the pith of the story more quickly: "your bottle of whisky sent one man to the White House and the other to a drunkard's grave."

HANDY COBBLER.

SAVE YOUR MONEY AND TIME

By Mending Your Shoes, Boots, Harness, Rubber Boots and Coats, Wire Fences, and do a Hundred Odd Jobs at Home with Our Cobbling Outfit.

Premium No. 68.

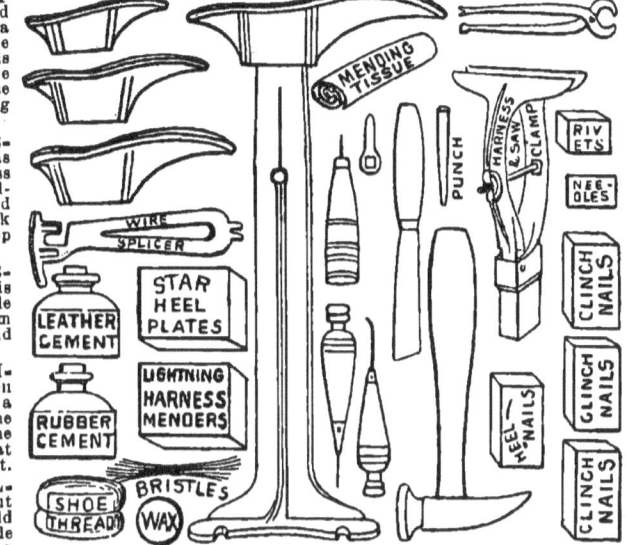

MANY A BOOT OR SHOE would last longer if it had a little patching done to it, and yet it is thrown away because of the inconvenience and expense of taking it to the shoemaker.

MANY A RUBBER BOOT has been rendered useless by reason of a nail-hole in the sole, and you never could think to take it to the shop for repair.

MANY A RUBBER COAT is made uncomfortable by a leak in the seam and nothing at hand to stop it.

MANY AN ACCIDENT has been caused by having a defective strap in the harness because the means were not at hand for repairing it.

MANY A DOLLAR is paid out for repairs that could just as well be made at home, and many a dollar is lost by putting off needed repairs, awaiting a convenient time to go to the shop.

MANY DISCOMFORTS, inconveniences and losses such as the above can be avoided by having about a Handy Cobbler, a complete outfit for repairing boots, shoes, rubber boots, rubber coats, harness, wire fences and a hundred of odd jobs around home.

NO ONE CAN AFFORD TO WASTE MONEY at any time, Therefore, you should not waste a moment waiting to send for this handy outfit. It will soon pay for itself.

The following are the articles the outfit contains, with their retail prices:

4 Iron Lasts...................$1.50	1 Box Lightning Menders .20	1 Dozen Bristles................. .05
1 Iron Standard............... .50	4 Packages Shoe-nails....... .40	4 Harness-needles, assorted .05
1 Shoe-hammer............... .15	6 Pairs Heel-plates............ .30	1 Harness and Saw Clamp... 1.00
1 Shoe-knife..................... .25	1 Bottle Rubber Cement.... .25	1 Leather-punch .... .25
1 Sewing-awl.................... .10	1 Bottle Leather Cement... .25	1 Box Rivets...................... .20
1 Harness-awl.................. .15	1 Ball Shoe-thread............ .05	1 Pair Wire-nippers .... .25
1 Pegging-awl.................. .25	1 Ball Shoemaker's Wax.... .05	1 Package Mending-tissue. .25

Every article in the outfit is made from first-class material.

PREMIUM No. 68.—Given as a premium for a club of 8 yearly subscribers to Farm and Fireside at the regular price, 50 cents a year.
Price, when purchased, $2.75; or with Farm and Fireside one year, $3.

PREMIUM No. 90.—This Cobbling Outfit is exactly the same as the one described above, except that it does not contain the harness tools. In this outfit there are 26 articles.
Premium No. 90 given as a premium for a club of 5 yearly subscribers to Farm and Fireside at the regular price, 50 cents a year.
Price, when purchased, $1.75; or with Farm and Fireside one year, $2.

Shipping Directions Cobbling Outfit must be sent by freight or express, at the purchaser's expense. Go in with your neighbors and order five outfits. They can be sent by freight as cheap as a single outfit. By a special arrangement one outfit can be sent by express about as cheap as by freight. Give shipping directions.

MAST, CROWELL & KIRKPATRICK, Springfield, Ohio.

THE WONDERFUL
CHRISTY KNIVES

Given FREE for a Club of 4 Subscribers to
———— FARM AND FIRESIDE.

14 inches long by 1¼ inches wide.

Premium No. 29.

11⅞ inches long by 1 inch wide.

6⅞ inches long by ¾ inch wide.

Who has not heard of the wonderful Christy knives? Where is there a housekeeper who would do without them after they have once used them, or can find a fault with them? We do not know of any, for we have only heard words of praise for them from our readers who are so fortunate as to own a set. They are made of fine sheet steel, with a round steel handle fastened onto the knife so it cannot possibly come off. The wavy beveled edge is the secret of their superiority. They will cut hot, new bread in thin slices without a crumb. Wherever a knife is needed in kitchen and dining-room we guarantee these knives to give perfect satisfaction.

The Bread-knife While this is called the bread-knife, it can be used for any purpose where a strong, sharp knife is needed. It is the finest carving-knife to be had.

The Cake-knife Is simply perfection when it comes to cutting cake, as it will cut the most delicate frosting and the lightest cake without crushing it or scattering a single crumb.

The Paring-knife Is pronounced faultless by every lady who has tried it. It is the universal verdict that it is the best paring-knife ever invented.

PREMIUM No. 29.—Given as a premium for a club of 4 yearly subscribers to Farm and Fireside at the regular price, 50 cents a year.

Price, when purchased, $1.00; or with Farm and Fireside one year, $1.25.

Postage paid by us in each case.

Address FARM AND FIRESIDE,
SPRINGFIELD, OHIO.

www.ingramcontent.com/pod-product-compliance
Lightning Source LLC
Chambersburg PA
CBHW020141170426
43199CB00010B/828